CONNECTING

church&home

A GRACE-BASED PARTNERSHIP

DR. TIM KIMMEL

randall house

114 Bush Rd I Nashville, TN 37217
randallhouse.com

Then there's Darcy—the great synthesizer of some of the most profound features of God's love. If you had this book tested for fingerprints, hers would be all over it. I've thoroughly enjoyed doing our personal family ministry together with this amazing lady.

There's a reason why God's grace can't be embraced in the abstract; it's because it was delivered in person, on a cross, by the Son of God. And it's to Him that I offer the ultimate acknowledgement and glory.

DEDICATION

TO

KYLER WILLIAM KIMMEL

&

HAYES DAVIS KIMMEL

YOUNG GUNS OF A GREAT NEW FAMILY MINISTRY.

TABLE OF CONTENTS

CHAPTER 1

CHURCH FAMILY MINISTRY:
SUB-CONTRACTED PARENTHOOD

This is a book about starting at the right place. Some prefer to focus on the path we take or the destination we ultimately reach. Obviously these deserve their place in the sun—and we'll weigh in on them before we're done. But where we start—it's the more critical point. It defines our journeys as well as our objectives: whether it's raising a family, maintaining friendships, making a living or wasting time, etc.

And it definitely has the defining impact on how parents and churches team up to produce a new generation of passionate followers of Jesus.

That's why I want to begin with a definition, two, in fact. Since just about every word in the dictionary has multiple ways of being described, it's obvious that these definitions don't cover the totality of these two words. But they clearly help us dial in on the bigger discussion we're going to have in this book.

FAMILY: THE DOMESTIC CHURCH
CHURCH: A GATHERING OF DOMESTIC CHURCHES

Obviously some people appear to be flying solo when they show up for church. We like to call them "singles" but that's really an illusion. No one is truly single. Everyone is part of a family, regardless of how healthy it is (or was). Most of us that show up for church walk from the parking lot with the people we live with throughout the week. We represent the families that make up the shared body of our churches.

This book is about how a family leverages its collective assets to raise the spiritual stock value of its local church . . . and how a local church leverages its collective assets to raise the spiritual stock value of its families—and both of these done with the combined goal of enhancing God's power and presence within our culture. There's a reason why it would be nice if both families and churches got on the same page.

We need each other.

More important, God always expected us to. In fact, we were designed to operate in rhythm like dancers. Families and churches are the only two cradle-to-grave organisms in a Christian worldview. But busy churches and hurried families have gotten their respective bodies operating more like break dancers than as dance partners.

For most families, church is a line item on their schedules. That's fair, I guess. There are a lot of food, clothing, shelter, health, education, and welfare priorities that fill most of the other lines.

And for most churches, families, though highly valued, equally show up as a line item on its agenda. That's understandable, I guess. There are lots of evangelism, discipleship, marrying, burying, and caring for the hurting priorities that fill most of its other lines. These other priorities cause these two to intersect occasionally with each other.

Before you finish this book, I hope to show you how a deliberate partnership between families and churches will do more to enhance and fulfill these other priorities (line items) than any other efforts either of them can make individually.

I don't see the church as an entity having absolute authority over the family, nor do I see the family as an entity having absolute authority over the church. Both families and churches should be in submission to God. On most things, God gives the parents the final word on what's going on with their kids. On certain specific things, God gives the church the final word. And since one is really just a bigger extension of the other, it would be great if both allowed God to create a seamless strategy that helped each bring the best out of the other.

HISTORICAL DILEMMAS

It might seem like ancient history to go back 75 years, but let's frame our contemporary church/family dilemma inside a recent historical context. With the growth of America's industrial complex through the first half of the 20th century and the end of World War II, families moved *en masse* from rural settings to the suburbs. This migration changed the configuration of the average church and what it could offer its families.

Suburban churches grew in size, enabling them to afford a seminary-trained senior pastor, but also a seminary or Bible school-trained children and youth pastor. This began the era of spiritual specialization when it came to age-focused ministry. Not only did a church have a pastor with theological sophistication, but it could also supply other leaders, who also had the capacity to parse Greek and Hebrew verbs.

For most parents, it was just in time. The demands of a competitive marketplace, the rise of the basic standard of living, greater academic expectations, quantum leaps in technology, and easy access to new forms of information and entertainment meant that the ability for a parent to frame and manage their child's values and beliefs were suddenly up against monumental competition. Add to this the movement of both parents to the workforce, a protracted era of divorce, and the loss of childhood naïveté regarding the harsher sides of culture and parents suddenly felt like they were outgunned—especially in the area of spiritual priorities in their home.

No problem. They realized they had ecclesiastical professionals at church that had forgotten more about the Bible than both parents knew collectively. Add into the mix state-of-the-art programming with Pied-Piper level leadership and it was easy to assume those things being left blank at home could be filled in by the pros at church.

Without meaning to, the growth and sophistication of children and youth programs at churches unwittingly created a toxic co-dependency between families and churches. There was a time when parents knew that if they didn't take the point position in leading, teaching, and grooming their kids morally and spiritually, no one else would. Generations of parents armed only with the King James Bible and a huge spiritual commitment did just fine in passing on a spiritual legacy. With the growth of metropolitan churches, parents suddenly realized they had these amazing minds and tenderhearted leaders at church ready to carry the spiritual heavy water for them when it came to their kids.

Let's be very clear about spiritual leadership and training in the home. When it's done effectively, it requires a lot of time, commitment, and focus by the parent. But if you're already out of wind, out of ideas, and at your wits end emotionally, the professionals at church suddenly become more than someone you feel has your back. You'd prefer they have your job. Walking carefully and conscientiously by faith on behalf of one's children isn't impossible, but it's clearly demanding. Any time we can have someone come along and lighten our load—especially when we're feeling overwhelmed—it's real easy to get into the habit of handing him or her the entire load in the process.

It's one thing to become a careful student of the Bible on behalf of your children when you feel like you absolutely must. It's quite another thing to do it when you know you have such incredible horsepower to cover this base for you at church. Put the child in a Christian school and the inclination for the parent to want to hit the cruise control button on their biblical leadership and learning curve is even stronger.

All of this to say that little by little, parents began to sub-contract the spiritual heavy lifting to the professionals at church (and parochial schools). Feeling like this base was adequately covered, they could concentrate their attention on providing a better lifestyle and creating some fun memories. The parent's job shifted to offering occasional biblical sound bites and a full-time commitment to overseeing their children's spiritual report cards. The kids' religious lives became more of a performance over which mom or dad presided. The parent's focus became more about the child's outward behavior, sin-management, and spiritual image-control—the logical conclusion of a sub-contracted arrangement.

Too bad none of this actually works.

In the meantime, society went through some radical plastic surgery. The roles of men and women/husbands and wives went under the cultural knife. Too many kids moved from being offspring of their parents' love to extensions of their parents' egos. Marriage as an institution was sliced in two. A "Jesus Incorporated" mindset began to haunt churches as their main priorities moved from evangelism and discipleship to buildings, budgets, and behinds. Technology not only started to redefine the average kid, but control him as well. Parents became uniformly distracted from their higher biblical roles. And morals as *absolute* guidelines for living one's life joined telephones that actually plug into a wall as part of the past.

A NOD TO POSTMODERNISM

To <u>not</u> acknowledge the presence and influence of postmodernism as a major definer of this bigger picture of where we currently are is to deny the *obvious*. The assumption that a child or teenager coming to church today is even *inclined* to believe the gospel story—as it is typically presented—is the new naïveté. Old-school thinking assumes that the gospel story and all of its respective theological pieces are *self-evident*. "They're true because God says they're true and I say they're true." Sorry, but today's kids aren't hard-wired to buy that hermeneutic anymore. To be honest, most likely no kid has ever been born with a natural wiring to buy that hermeneutic. But there was a time when the culture surrounding us backed up the parents when we said that something was true "because I say it's true." However, we're now living in a postmodern era where the culture surrounding us validates our children's skepticism with its own refusal to recognize absolute truth.

Churches, either steeped in tradition or staffed to a pre-postmodern way of thinking, suddenly find themselves losing their voice to the next generation, while at the same time trying to figure out how to hold the hearts of their kids.

After two and a half generations of parents outsourcing their spiritual responsibilities to the evangelical "Special Forces" at church, family ministry leaders are finally suggesting that the parents start assuming their rightful position in the spiritual/biblical food chain. And there are a lot of parents that would like to take them up on this.

GOOGLE PARENTS

The problem is that helplessness and hopelessness tend to be the default mode when mom and dad actually consider whether or not to carry more of their assigned spiritual weight. Where we've been and where we are as families and churches has created more of a Google relationship between parents and God. Typical parents not only don't feel they know what they're doing when it comes to leading their kids spiritually, but they also assume the job is too complicated for it to ever be *intuitive*. What they want are answers from church leaders to specific problems without having to grasp any kind of a bigger picture. And the consumer mindset that has permeated many of the adult spectators showing up on Sunday morning inclines them to believe the answers to their family issues are what they deserve. It's what they've paid for with their offering.

Some churches accommodate this by programming with the assumption that the average parent is biblically limited and spiritually lame. Actually, this might be true for some of us, but certainly not the mainstream parent. Unfortunately, it causes family ministry leadership to assume a spoon-feeding relationship with mom and dad. Since people tend to rise to our expectations of them, parents get right in line for their weekly snack from their church's family ministry.

Where church was meant to be a sacred fitness center, it's now much more a giant halfway house and soup kitchen for families. Where family ministers were trained to be coaches, they more often find themselves as holy EMTs.

FROM ONE EXTREME TO ANOTHER

When something goes too far off course in one direction, it's not surprising for there to be a movement to correct the course that, unfortunately, sends everything too far off in the other direction. There is a well-intended movement that has risen out of the debris of the professional family ministry programming mindset at church and the sub-contracting mindset of parents. This movement feels that the best way to solve this problem is to eliminate any department or program at a church that mirrors the role of a parent or makes it easy for a parent not to carry out their God-given responsibility of spiritually leading their children. In other words, get rid of children's ministry and youth ministry departments at your church.

Part of me has great respect for people who want to make radical changes to fix an obvious problem. Cold turkey is one way to deal with addictions. But this knee-jerk reaction to a problem has its own shortcomings built into it that could well undermine the spiritual legacy of children just as much, if not more, than what we're currently dealing with. It also implies a limitation of the work of the Holy Spirit in our children's lives to one primary influence—the parent. Who are we to say the only way God ever meant for our children's beliefs and values to be framed was exclusively through their parents in general and their father in particular? So much for "the heavens declare the glory of God"[1] and all of those wonderfully gifted people God gave to the church (both local and domestic) "from him the whole body, joined and held together by every supporting ligament, grows and builds itself up in love, as each part does its work."[2]

And just because you don't have a "formal" children's or youth program in your church doesn't mean you don't still have those departments. If parents are taking their children to a local church (which God has commanded them to do), and . . .

† Some wiser woman assists them with a struggling, uncomfortable child
† Or anyone else speaks truth or encouragement into their children
† Or the pastor formally teaches their children through his sermon
† Or some other dad comes alongside them to help them with a difficult teenager
† Or the collective body prays for their children's spiritual journey

Then that church has children's and youth ministry whether it wants to call it such or not. And those parents are utilizing a children and youth ministry influence from their church, whether they want to admit it or not.

One of the major goals of this book is to help parents step up their game when it comes to being the primary spiritual influencer in their children's lives. But God has a lot of ways He can and does orchestrate the finished product. He can use all kinds of threads to create the final faith tapestry of our children—including the loving people who come alongside us at church to help build a spiritual legacy into our kids. So, since any parent taking their kids to a local church is exposing them to a *de facto* children's ministry and youth ministry—whether we want to call it such or not—it might make sense to make sure those ministries are operating intentionally rather than accidentally.

And to the credit of this response and movement, it's prompting a long overdue discussion. Some churches need to be prepared to make radical changes to how they view their formal family ministry. They may not need to throw the whole concept under a bus driven by reaction, but careful scrutiny of what they're doing could well yield a lot of great improvement of the church/family mambo.

BACK TO WHERE WE STARTED

Let's go back to our definition. A family is supposed to be "the domestic church." It's the smallest church out there. Dads and moms are supposed to be the pastors and pastorettes of a full-blown, albeit tiny, freestanding ecclesia. Their job is to do the work of the ministry throughout the week in their children's lives and then make sure they bring their family to church on *full* rather than *empty* when Sunday comes around.

The church ("a collection of domestic churches") is supposed to come alongside mom and dad as an ally, mentor, and cheerleader. It's supposed to be there to help answer the more sophisticated biblical and theological questions. And it's supposed to be there to help families through the tougher seasons of life. So, the church does its normal teaching and training, but it's supposed to be in complement to what's happening at home, not in place of.

It might help to stop and acknowledge the obvious:
Strong churches don't make strong families.
Strong families make strong churches.

Once a church figures this out—from senior pastor, bishops, elders, deacons, and on through—things change. And once we parents figure this out, somebody better bar the door! The business-as-usual mindset that invites the church to supplant the parent's God-ordained role suddenly comes to a screeching halt. It stops because everyone finally recognizes the truth of the business-as-usual mindset: *it isn't working.*

It can't work because it's configured contrary to God's design.

You can throw all the money and personnel at your family ministry department you want. You can create the biggest dog-and-pony show in family ministry history. It's just going to go right into the sinkhole.

Obviously, there are some issues that must be dealt with in our families. And there will always be a part of the church that must function as an emergency room for the broken and battered. But what we must get serious about is moving to a mindset that not only recognizes the biblical role of our parents, but also believes that God is big enough, His Word is clear enough, and His Spirit is powerful enough to come alongside standard believing parents and give them what they need to do their job well.

WIN/WIN

We need to realize the truth: that the deliberate efforts of a lay-level parent, who only brings a passionate love for Jesus and a passionate desire to pass that love on to their children, can eclipse the most sophisticated efforts of the best seminary-trained professional a church could find. When both parents and churches get on this same page, the spiritual stock value of our domestic churches and local churches is going to see a radical spike. Churches will be able to do their job better and with more positive outcome, and parents will win as well.

And here's the coolest thing of all: God has given both the parents and the church a unifying and complete starting point for everything that follows in the parent/church dance of family ministry—His grace! It's the same place He starts with each of us as He enters our lives and transforms our hearts. As I said at the beginning of this chapter, our starting point determines everything!

Before we're done, we're going to see how God's grace can not only define but also direct how parents love and lead their kids and how churches love and lead their families.

It's a grace-based family ministry mindset that is a direct extension of God's heart. And it's the best way for churches and parents to join hands with God to bring Jesus home.

ENDNOTES

[1] Psalm 19:1.

[2] Ephesians 4:16.

CHAPTER 2

HOMEGROWN FAITH

M any years ago, my wife and I were volunteering in the nursery at our church. They wanted Darcy because she actually had some clue what little infants and toddlers needed. They wanted me to help Darcy. I spent a lot of time on the floor playing with the kids and then rocking them to sleep when they got tired.

I remember two different sets of parents who brought their babies and left them in our care. We knew both couples well. They were friends of ours. But what we knew about them and how each processed the Christian life gave us excitement over the future of one of the babies left in our care and concern over the other.

Both sets of parents believed in Jesus. Both were committed to raising their kids to believe in Him too. And both sets of parents were excited to raise up their children in close connection to our church. This is where the similarities ended. When it came to the role they wanted our church to play in the bigger picture of their family, the two couples came from opposite points of view.

The one couple took their faith personally and seriously. Both were motivated by an obvious heart connection they had with Jesus. They felt they were the ones primarily responsible for their child's spiritual maturity. The focused goal in their life was to *trust*

God for everything. They believed God wouldn't have assigned kids to their care if He didn't think they were capable, through His power, to raise them up to love Him and care for other people. This couple saw our church as a wonderful extension of all they were doing in their home. They appreciated the teaching, the worship, the friendships, and the encouragement. They saw our church as their ally, prompter, and standard-setter for a higher commitment to loving each other and leading their kids.

The other mom and dad were two very nice people, but they saw our church more as their spiritual life-support system. They depended on it to prop them up and keep them going spiritually. They didn't feel God could actually empower them to be the spiritual standard-bearers for their children. They simply felt too inadequate. They felt their primary goal was to *obey* God and to get their kids to obey Him too. They measured their spiritual maturity based on how well they were able to jump through the proper evangelical hoops. They depended on the church to tell them what to do, which explains why their focus as Christian parents was mostly on getting proper spiritual behavior from their kids rather than building a spiritual disposition (that organically leads to heart led obedience). Unfortunately, they tended to bring their kids to church spiritually undernourished Sunday after Sunday and expected the various pastors and volunteers to top their tanks.

I've had the chance now to watch both kids grow up. They both went to the same Sunday school classes, the same worship services, the same VBS programs, the same camps, and the same youth groups. They were taught the exact same biblical stories, doctrinal truths, and life applications. But their spiritual levels of maturity, biblical understanding, and confidence in God ended up light years apart. As young adults, these kids mirror—not the church they grew up in (because it was the same)—but the families they grew up in. The child, who had parents ready to carry the living water at home, was the one who hit the ground running as an adult. The other child turned out to be as equally codependent on the church as his parents.

What's interesting is that these two kids are now to the childbearing point in their lives. They'll bring their children to the nursery where people like Darcy and me will be waiting. Because of how they were raised, more than likely, they'll simply repeat the cycle for another generation.

WHOSOEVER WILL

Okay, let's acknowledge the obvious. There's nothing new about parents coming to church with radically different spiritual capacities when it comes to raising their kids. Lots of factors play into why that happens, and some of those factors have nothing to do with mistakes the parents are making. And the "whosoever will, may come" nature of the gospel will always guarantee that as a church we'll be welcoming families who run the gamut of spiritual and biblical IQs.

In addition, what churches do when it comes to programs will have little effect in changing the spiritual finished product of these families if they do *nothing* to reframe the thinking of both the parents and the church leaders. This is especially so if we see the primary role of the family ministry in our churches as one of teaching the Bible, doctrine, and Christian moral living to children. Chuck Swindoll made this point when he said, "life makes up its mind at home".[1] For the most part, life doesn't make up its mind at church, school, or work. These all do influence our thinking, and church can certainly help a person make up his or her mind about Jesus as Savior as well as about certain great truths pertaining to Him. But everything we learn is tempered and then interpreted within the more familial context in which we've been raised.

Obviously, kids can break free of bad contextual thinking without their parents going through a biblical makeover. But they are the exception rather than the rule. In most cases, they are the rare exception. So, if our churches are going to go to the trouble of having a family ministry, if we're going to spend the money on trained evangelical professionals to oversee it and the programs to fill it, if we're going to invest in the buildings and equipment needed to pull it off, does it make sense to have a family ministry whose *primary* role and goal is just to present quality programs supplemented by crafts, cookies, and take home papers?

Most gatekeepers of churches would never want to admit their family ministry is mainly a bunch of good programs, and that their family minister is functioning as little more than a program director on an evangelical cruise ship. I'd go as far as to say that most gatekeepers of churches would *assume* what they're doing is designed to have a transforming impact on their families as well as bolster what their families are doing at home when it comes to spiritual leadership. And it may do some of that accidentally. But if we want to do it deliberately, it requires a bigger view of the role of both the parents and the people framing the family ministries at our churches.

The numbers don't lie. Christian families are hurting. Parents are struggling to find their biblical roles, and the kids are the biggest losers in all of this. They are walking away from a faith that didn't or couldn't imprint them during its weekly two hour window into their lives. Churches and families have put themselves in a Catch-22 situation. Parents are expecting churches to come through for their kids, and churches are pulling out all of the stops to do it. But the harder parents push the more churches try, the less effective either is. Maybe we should take the advice of the old saying, "When riding a dead horse, for heaven's sake dismount!"

FROM THE SHORES OF TRIPOLI

Several years ago, I presided over the funeral of a great warrior of World War II, Brig. General Joe Foss. In fact, Joe had received the Congressional Medal of Honor for his amazing and courageous exploits as a Marine aviator in the Battle of Guadalcanal.

Because of the magnitude of Joe's personal profile as a warrior, statesman, and entertainer, lots of dignitaries, politicos, celebrities, and military brass from all over the country showed up to bid him farewell. Among those who came was Gen. William L "Spider" Nyland,[2] at that time the Assistant Commandant of the United States Marine Corps. It was Gen. Nyland who had been handpicked to deliver the eulogy on behalf of the Corps. Before he moved into his reflections, he said, "The purpose of the Marine Corps is to train Marines, to win America's wars, and to send a good citizen back into society." He went on to offer a touching review and salute to Joe Foss' great life.

As soon as he made his over-arching statement about the Marine Corps, I immediately thought to myself, "*No wonder they're so effective! They have such a clear and uncompromising vision of what they are trying to accomplish, and all of their effectiveness stems from that starting place.*" If you're a commissioned officer or NCO in the Marine Corps, you know exactly what you are trying to accomplish every moment of your waking hours. "I'm always training Marines. When it's time for us to engage our enemies, we're not going to *fight* them; we're going to *defeat* them. And everything I'm doing through my example as well as through my influence on my fellow Marines is purposed to send a good citizen back into society."

The Marine Corps has a lot of great programs. When it comes to teaching soldiers how to maintain their gear, fire their weapon, perform hand-to-hand combat, follow orders, and work as a unit, their programs are as good as you could ask for. The Marine Corps has phenomenal facilities and equipment too. And everyone knows the Corps' reputation for both commissioned and non-commissioned officers. But it's not its programs, facilities, equipment, or leadership that make it effective; it is its overall vision of what those programs, facilities, equipment, and leadership are supposed to accomplish that makes it effective. Everything the Corps is doing is about training Marines, winning America's wars, and sending good citizens back into society.

There may be times when it fell short, but those aren't indictments against these goals but more statements about individual Marines or outside interference from other government agencies. The historical record of the United States Marine Corps is all anyone needs to see in order to conclude that their over-arching goals are not only excellent, but they've also served the Corps and the United States well.

Keep in mind too that the USMC accomplishes those three goals through men and women who show up at the Marine Corps Recruit Depots in San Diego or Parris Island with little-to-no clue what being a Marine is all about, how to win *anything*, and often with a nondescript record as a citizen. But they are transformed by the clear vision put before them and subsequently prepared to carry out that vision by the various programs, facilities, equipment, and leaders the Marines have for them.

Because of my role as a family advocate, who equips parents on how to raise their kids in the power of God's grace, I often find myself in a church to conduct a parenting conference. Pastors and family pastors are typically my hosts. Naturally I'm very interested in what they are doing when it comes to family ministry. When I inquire, the standard responses I receive are:

† We have a phenomenal children's facility.

† We have a state-of-the-art check-in system that has really ramped up our levels of security.

+ We just installed some new playground equipment with misting machines for our hot summers.

+ This fall we instituted a couple's getaway that has been well received. We're definitely going to make it an annual event.

+ We're very proud of this wonderful curriculum we have that loops a child through a complete overview of the Bible and systematic theology three times between their birth and their graduation from high school.

+ Our junior high and high school departments have individual gathering areas that are so unique, so clever. Man, the adults are jealous of the kind of facilities we've supplied for them. It's a real crowd pleaser.

+ You won't believe the lay staff God has sent to us. We have a woman, who graduated from Yale, overseeing our elementary school department.

In the same way, parents outline their goals for passing on their Christian faith to their kids with lists of their programs:

+ We have our kid in a Christian school.

+ Our son attends AWANA.

+ We have family devotions five mornings a week.

+ We signed our daughter up for VBS at three churches this summer.

+ Each of our children has his or her own Bible with his or her name engraved on it.

It would be like me asking Gen. Nyland to tell me about his beloved Marine Corps and he takes off about their latest version of night vision goggles and the new dining hall they had installed at Camp Pendleton with its 15 flavored cappuccino kiosks. Sorry, that wouldn't come out of his mouth. Instead I'd hear something like, "Tim, I'm so proud of the wonderful men and women who are working so hard at all our installations around the world. They are the finest soldiers that have ever worn our proud uniform. Tim, we are currently engaged in three theaters of combat, and we have a strategy that we know will guarantee us complete victory. And I love the chance we're having in these soldiers' lives to groom them to take on positive and significant roles in their communities once they complete their service to their Corps. We always want our Marines to be an asset to their country as long as they live." His vision captures the *heart* of what they're doing not just the *task* of what they're doing.

Don't get me wrong, I love to see the innovative facilities and hear about the latest ways to transfer solid teaching to kids and their parents. I love to hear of the different things parents might be doing to help their kids on their spiritual journey.

But I go back to the two babies dropped off at the nursery so long ago. They enjoyed all of the innovations and best-of-the-best teaching that our church could offer, but how it played out in their lives was primarily determined by how their parents saw *their* role. It seems that churches often struggle with an inflated view of their two hour-a-week influence on the family and parents often struggle with a limited view of their seven-day-a-week influence on their kids.

Parents, who depend on the church to do the bulk of the spiritual heavy lifting, are seldom satisfied. No matter how much a church spends or how much their staff and volunteers try, parents who are co-dependent will always feel the church could have or should have done more. This can be extremely discouraging for the wonderful people who serve so sacrificially to love on those parents and their kids.

BIG PICTURE, CLEARER VISION

When I think of my role as a parent, it's easy to get lost in the individual pieces of my job. Even if I limited the discussion to my spiritual role, there are still a lot of moving parts that could weigh down my resolve. That's why I prefer always to have a big picture in mind. It gives me 20/20 vision when it's time to actually get up in the morning and live around my kids.

In the same way, when churches have a comprehensive "big picture" understanding of what they are trying to accomplish, it's so much easier to align people, programs, and facilities to their highest and best capacity. It's also easier to move parents from an out-sourcing or codependent mindset to a fully engaged commitment to pastor their personal domestic church.

Let me suggest a big picture, spiritual role of a parent that can get your creative juices moving. Hopefully, it can stir up a healthy discussion between church leadership and parents as you both consider how to best minister to your families.

The role of a parent is to connect to the *heart* of his or her child in such a way he or she prepares that child to more easily connect to the heart of God.

Notice I didn't say teach them the Bible, pray with them, take them to church, teach them to obey, discipline them, make sure they know good doctrine, and have a biblical worldview. These are all great "parts" of the bigger picture. They all have a place within the on-going spiritual responsibilities of a Christian parent. But they can be transferred academically or by memory without a heart connection to the child and ultimately have very little impact on the finished spiritual product. Without a heart connection, these "parts" are little more than exercises and information. It is within the context of a *heart relationship* that these vital spiritual tools have an influence on the divine grit and spiritual resolve of a child.

When I say "heart connection," I'm not referring to the obvious and assumed love that parents have for their children. Nor am I talking about the assumed love that children have for their parents. I'm talking about a level of relationship that is so deeply felt in the heart it automatically inclines the people involved towards mutual honor, joy, respect, appreciation, and the desire to consistently pursue the other person's good. My hope is that before you close the back cover of this book, you'll understand exactly how this is attained.

Why do I suggest that the overarching strategy start with a heart connection? I don't want to be a name-dropper, but it's how *God* does it with us. There are lots of people, living and dead, who could make straight A's on biblical exams, theological reviews, and biblical worldview debates yet have (or had) little-to-no sense of an intimacy with God which would naturally drive them to a passionate love for their fellow man. Assuming the right information is all it takes to set people up for spiritual success is naïve and doesn't jive with the biblical narrative. James 2:19 says, "You believe that there is one God. Good! Even the demons believe that—and shudder!" Applying this verse to our discussion here, the point is: Orthodox theology is a good thing, but don't assume that it, by itself, is going to do the job for you, especially when it comes to your family. The demons believe orthodox theology (and it scares the junk out of them), but they're still *demons!*

When parents consistently embody the heart of God's love, mercy, and grace, then all of the other spiritual exercises take hold—not just in their child's intellect, but in their emotions and spirit as well.

With this in mind, what should the bigger vision for a church's family ministry look like? Once again, I offer you a *suggestion* not as a final word, but as a catalyst to get you thinking more deliberately about this vision and then dreaming as parents and church leaders on what this would look like.

The goal of a church's family ministry is to connect to the *heart* of each individual family leader in such a way that it better prepares those parents to develop a heart connection to their kids that subsequently inclines those kids towards a deeper love for the Lord and kindness toward others.

This doesn't diminish the individual role that a family ministry plays in children or young people's lives. It doesn't mean we no longer need things like VBS, youth group, or children's church. It just shifts its emphasis to a higher focus on the impact it has on the true ministers to the children of the church—their parents. This better defines not only the parental training that a family ministry offers, but also the priority it places on it. This overarching vision sets up a church to have a much more effective impact on all of the family members. It also puts the church in the best position to create a comprehensive plan for maintaining that heart connection not only by what it teaches them, but also by *how* it teaches them.

And, once again, I've got good news: God's grace offers what we need to make this happen.

ENDNOTES

[1] Chuck Swindoll, *Home: Where Life Makes Up Its Mind* (Portland: Multnomah Press, 1980) p. 6.

[2] Gen. William Nyland gave the US Marine Corps 37 years of distinguished service. He retired in 2005. Joe Foss was a Marine aviator in the battle for control of the skies over the island of Guadalcanal in World War II. Joe died January 1, 2003.

CHAPTER 3

A PLAN THAT WORKS

S tarbucks is a verb: "I need to Starbucks my face" (which refers to the effect a certain blend of coffee has on a person's taste buds and attitude). Starbucks started out as a noun: "I need to take my face to Starbucks" (which refers to the place where a person goes to affect their taste buds and attitude). Before that, Starbucks wasn't even a word. For most of my life, if someone had said the word *Starbucks*, I wouldn't have had a clue of what they were talking about. Unless you're familiar with the first mate on the whale ship *Pequod* in Melville's classic, *Moby Dick*, you probably hadn't heard the word either. Now, it's an anchor tenant of our vocabulary.

If someone thinks Starbucks is about coffee, they'd be wrong. Serving an excellent cup of coffee obviously plays a huge part in what happens at Starbucks. The bulk of the money they make is a result of tens of millions of people who willingly pay Starbucks enormous amounts of money for a cup of coffee . . . day in day out, year after year. If we went to Starbucks' corporate headquarters, we'd find a significant part of it committed to the on-going maintenance and development of their various coffee brands. So Starbucks sells tons of coffee, yet they aren't about coffee. The fact is there are lots of places you can go to get a great cup of coffee—and a lot cheaper too. So why is it so many people choose to pay more to buy their coffee at Starbucks? It's because it's not about coffee.

Let's keep this exercise going just a bit longer to make a point. Is Starbucks about food? No. They have a lot of options for fun things to eat, and they make trainloads of money each day from all the food they sell, but food isn't what they're about.

How about entertainment? This might be getting a little closer to what they're about, but if by saying "entertainment" we're referring to the musical CDs/downloads, movie DVDs, and books they sell then, nope, that's not what Starbucks is *about* either.

Starbucks is about "experience"—the human experience. It might be a retired man who goes there to get his daily kick-you-in-the-head cup of bold blend as he reads the morning paper. It's often kids meeting after school or in the evening to do homework *together*. Lots of business takes place at Starbucks. Deals are sealed, people are hired, and people get fired sitting in the comfortable ambience of Starbucks. And a lot of love happens and unhappens at Starbucks. It's where couples have started their relationship and many have called it quits. Starbucks is also a great place to think, even by yourself. The latte they mix up for you might cost them at the most, pennies on the dollar. The extra $3.50 is the rent you're paying for the human experience.

STARBUCKS COMMUNITY CHURCH

There are lots of reasons why people go to church. It might be tradition, guilt, a sense of duty, to fill a void, to serve, it's Christmas, it's Easter, or it might actually be driven by a genuine love for the God the church represents.

Why do people go to a particular church? You have all the reasons just mentioned plus many more, like: it's the church they grew up in, they enjoy the pastor or the style of worship, their friends go there, they feel safe there, or it's their denomination of choice.

Why do churches even exist? If you pose this question to

pastors, who came out of evangelical seminaries, their answer most often aligns with the two marching orders they received on graduation day: evangelism and discipleship. Although these are their primary marching orders, most churches have "features" that are more often the real reasons people go to them. These features tend to consume the greater passions of its leadership. There are churches famous for their worship experience or the charm and kindness of their pastor. Some stand out for their commitment to the careful teaching of the Bible, some for the children's or youth department, some for their emphasis on missions, some for their active ministry to the poor and underserved, some for their facilities, and some for their hipness. There's nothing wrong with any of these being outstanding features of a church. All of them can be excellent vehicles for churches to evangelize and disciple followers of Christ.

A THREE-DIMENSIONAL APPROACH

Let's go back to Starbucks for a second and let me introduce two words to our discussion: *strategy* and *tactics*. Starbucks is a business that knows it has to make a profit in order to continue to exist. It has a *strategy* to do this and *tactics* to carry out the strategy. The *strategy* involves creating an ambience through its facilities and the kind of service offered that inclines people to come in droves and spend a lot of money on flavored water. Starbucks has carefully calculated *tactics* to carry out its strategy. These include the color palate of the store, the comfort of the furniture, free Wi-Fi, the disarming personality of employees, the variety and quality on the coffee menu, the customization of your order, and the intimate touch added by using your first name when you get your drink. There's a sense of coffee *theater* that makes up part of the experience.

Starbucks also tries hard to be a great place to be employed. Letting part-timers be shareholders and providing strong healthcare benefits are just some of the ways Starbucks stands out from the competition. Customers, employees, and community are all part of the strategy and tactics of Starbucks.

A local church isn't a business (although some of its detractors would argue with that point). Churches must operate with good business practices because they employ people and steward God's resources. But their existence isn't as a profit center. A local church is primarily a gathering together of God's family members in order to accomplish a greater good. Yet, just like Starbucks, there's *strategy* and *tactics* determining how churches operate.

Take any of the other "features" listed earlier and you can see how they require strategy and tactics to pull them off. Each strategy can have the exact same goals—to draw people to Jesus in salvation and then align them closer to His image through discipleship. There are churches that do this through worship, strong Bible teaching, missions, community service, liturgy, or being contemporarily *cool*. The number of people who show up week after week often is the standard used to measure how effective a church is. But anybody in his or her right biblical mind knows that database is a "human" way of measuring success that may or may not have any bearing on whether a church is truly effective. God can use all kinds of features, all sizes of churches, and all measures of giftedness to do His bidding. And, like coffee shops, just because a lot of people are crowded in to it doesn't mean it offers the best cup of java in town.

The fact is, you can have two churches within a block of each other using the exact same strategy and tactics and yet God's power to imprint and transform is obvious in one and hard to find in the other. Their staff can come from the exact same schools, their demographic can be from the exact same pool of people, yet the impact of the one might eclipse that of the other in astounding ways.

What's going on then?

Let me introduce a third word to our discussion that can help answer that question: *philosophy*. When I'm around church leadership I tend to hear a lot of strategic type of talk. That's how leaders talk. They're constantly thinking about how they can get gifted people, provide them with the resources they need in the right setting, and then leverage all of it to accomplish a greater goal (which is usually measured by how many people show up for these strategic endeavors). When I'm around the rank and file church attendee, I hear more tactical talk. They're basically saying, "Tell me what to do, and I'll do it." They want whatever they get from church to be practical and easy to implement—even if it only gets them through the moment.

Here's what's interesting. Whether you think strategically or tactically, there's a philosophy determining the effectiveness of the strategy and tactics you're taking. The leader and follower might not be able to articulate the philosophy behind their thinking, but it's still there. And once they find out what that philosophy is, they might not want to admit it, but it's still the philosophy driving their strategy or tactics.

ASKING HARD QUESTIONS

So, what if the philosophy is flawed? The answer is something no one wants to hear; yet it's still true. Flawed *philosophy* creates flawed *strategy*, which leads people to embrace flawed *tactics*. Notice I'm saying "flawed." I'm not saying "wrong" or "evil." The strategy and tactics are *flawed*. They might be flawed because the philosophy behind them is incomplete, or it's too heavily ruled by human conclusions, or it's framed from someone's personal inadequacies, or it's the reaction to some other flawed philosophy. And although a lot of people might be involved in mobilizing the church's strategies and implementing its tactics, it's not necessarily coming close to what it could be if it had a truer and more overarching philosophy.

A philosophy, for instance, that is completely aligned with God's heart.

Everything I'm saying about how a church ministers to its people goes across the board to how parents minister to their kids. A person or church's philosophy is a combination of two things rattling around at the philosophical starting point of their thinking: presuppositions and perspectives. Presuppositions actually shape our personal perspective. Both of them write the script of our philosophy—whether it's about God, love, marriage, parenting, work, play, money, or sex.

So, the smart guys behind the green-circled logo decided they wanted to make a bunch of money selling coffee. Their presupposition and perspective (philosophy) on their customer was that people are living out a huge human drama. It's a drama that runs the gauntlet from comedy to tragedy. Regardless of where they are on that human continuum, people like to have a common and comfortable place to experience their drama. They also love to accompany whatever kind of drama they're experiencing with a cup of the universal drug of choice in their hand. And they'd prefer it if the person handing them their coffee actually appears to *care* about them. These corporate guys figured they could most likely sell an ocean of coffee if they provided this kind of ideal context for humans to experience their individual and collective dramas. And I tend to believe their success was because they genuinely care about their customer.

Thus, Starbucks.[1]

Dr. Ken Boa, has a profound way of summarizing this: "Your presuppositions *will* shape your perspectives [philosophy], your perspectives *will* shape your priorities [strategy], your priorities *will* shape your performance [tactics]."[2]

What if the presuppositions and perspectives behind a church's philosophy are that people are primarily hurting, they exist in a fairly beaten down frame of mind most of the time, their ability to grasp sophisticated nuances of theology is limited, and their capacity to take much responsibility for their personal lives is suspect? If this is the overarching philosophy of why that particular church exists, then most likely its strategy (priorities) is going to look like a gigantic spiritual and emotional emergency room. Most likely, the handfuls of healthy people serving in this ecclesiastical ER are going to wear out fast. The effectiveness of their efforts is going to depend on the willingness of the people they're treating to hold the spiritual or biblical band-aid on their wounded lives long enough for it to do any good.

I'm exaggerating to make a point—but not by much.

Let's say a church's strategy is to provide a highly controlled environment for families to safely church its children. It may have a school for the kids in place of public school or a church-wide commitment to homeschooling. It passes up opportunities to team with other evangelical churches, conferences, or camps that mix in kids from a more "pedestrian" type of family backgrounds. A high level of emphasis is placed on proper biblical knowledge, doctrine, and worldview as benchmarks of spiritual sophistication. Families are urged to limit their kids' music, arts, and entertainment exposure to outlets that pass a fairly stringent, spiritual litmus test. Christian behavior is articulated in very specific ways—even to the way young people dress, fix their hair, socialize, and serve. Parents are encouraged to do tighter policing of their children's personal lives and be ready to take quick and bold measures to protect or redirect them when they happen to stray off course. To make this more of a community strategy, the families are kept together more than they are separated when they are actually at church.

Let's call this church a "safe church." The presuppositions and perspectives behind its philosophy might have a lot to do with some bad experiences that its primary founders and influential adults had growing up in unchurched families. Perhaps they bore a lot of scar tissue from the culture that surrounded them before they came to know Christ. Or maybe they were part of a church that took no spiritual stands and gave no absolute moral direction—leaving people at the mercy of the forces of darkness. Or maybe they were brought up in a safe spiritual environment and want to reduplicate it for their kids. Or maybe they just see the propensity toward weakness and dumb choices inherent within the human condition and believe Christians need more external structure to stay on point. Actually, all of these can be legitimate issues that church leaders and parents take into account when they lay out the strategy and tactics of their family ministry.

And I'd even suggest that this type of church or the "Spiritual ER" church and the "Bible Teaching" church would be quick to say their ultimate desire is for people to know God personally (evangelism) and then grow in their relationship with Him (discipleship). Evangelism and discipleship is the generic *goal* of their strategy and tactics. But it's not necessarily the presuppositions and perspectives at the core of their philosophy.

The philosophies defining the strategies and tactics of these churches are that people are unsafe in their culture and need protected, or are in great stress and have cares that need to be met, or are limited in their knowledge of God and need more teaching to strengthen their commitment. Yet if these are the sum total of the philosophies fueling their strategies and tactics, the parents involved and the leaders at the helm might be real disappointed in the outcome of all of their sacrificial efforts.

Why? Because God's starting point with us is *relationship*. Sure, He sees our human condition, our cultural vulnerability and our limited understanding of Him and wants to play an eternal role in addressing these issues. But His primary motivation towards doing anything for us or to us is His love. "For God so loved the world that he gave his one and only Son, that whoever believes in him [the context is not assuming mere intellectual belief but belief that is connected through relationship], shall not perish but have eternal life" (John 3:16, brackets added). Life and love can't be experienced in a vacuum or in isolation. They are experienced in relational connection to someone else. God gave His Son so that we would have life and have it more abundantly. Life isn't abundant just because our physical needs are met, or we're safe from cultural threats, or we're biblically astute. Therefore, the philosophical starting point of our family ministry strategies and tactics must embody the relational desires of God's heart.

DIALED INTO GOD'S HEART

God desires to have an intimate relationship with people. He primarily creates and maintains that relationship through the qualities and character of His grace. Regardless of a person's condition, God can do marvelous things in, on, for, and through him or her when that person allows Him to turn him or her into living extensions of His heart of grace.

Grace is the distinctive word that defines the Word, Jesus of Nazareth. The grace of God was upon Him as He grew up (Luke 2:40). He was filled with grace (John 1:14). And even though there are many other wonderful attributes that define His divine make-up like truth, holiness, justice, and mercy, the word *grace* is the one that summarizes His loving nature and includes by definition His truth, holiness, justice, and mercy.

Regardless of the filters through which you interpret the Bible, there's a reason why theologians don't refer to the era we're living in as the covenant of truth or the dispensation of orthodoxy. They refer to it as either the covenant of grace or the dispensation of grace. We are saved by grace (Ephesians 2:8-9). Grace is not only the relational doorway to God's heart, but it's also the feature of His relationship with us that He consistently uses to maintain closeness to our hearts.

Let me bring in a heavy hitter, Dr. Lawrence O. Richards. Here's what he says about the transforming nature of God's grace:

> The grace affirmed in the NT (New Testament) is always mediated by Jesus. This grace is a dynamic force that does more than affect our standing with God by crediting us with righteousness. Grace affects our experience as well.
>
> In Romans 6, Paul traces something of the transforming impact of grace. He shows that when we are united with Jesus, we are removed from the realm of law, with its emphasis on works, and are established in the realm of grace. Grace is marked always by God's enabling work within us to overcome our helplessness. We yield ourselves to God and trust him to do what we are unable to do. This walk of faith releases us from the domination of sin, and we become slaves to God, doing his will and reaping the benefit of holiness.
>
> Romans 6 shows us that grace is not simply a basic orientation to relationship with God. It is also a practical approach to living the Christian life . . . .
>
> The biblical concept of grace is much greater than is suggested in the common definition of 'unmerited favor.' 'Grace' is a word that expresses a radical view of life and of relationship with God.
>
> Grace teaches that God's attitude toward us is one of acceptance and love; knowing God's heart, we can 'approach the throne of grace with confidence' (Heb. 4:16) with every sin and need.

Grace is a dramatic statement about the human condition. Each person is helpless, trapped in sin and incapable of pleasing God or winning his favor . . .

Grace is a way of life. Relying totally on Jesus to work within us, we experience God's own unlimited power, vitalizing us and enabling us to live truly good lives.[3]

Therefore, regardless of whether your family or your church's "family ministry" is built around strategy and tactics that address Christians' need for care, protection or biblical knowledge, if it is not philosophically launched from a desire to both experience God's heart of grace through relationship with Him and then live His grace out through how we treat each other, it will probably struggle to come close to reaching it's ultimate goal of effectively drawing people to Him (evangelism) and living in fellowship with him (discipleship).

Philosophy defines strategies that dictate tactics. The philosophical starting point of God's relationship with us was to love us through the power of His grace. His strategy is to sustain His relationship with us through the ongoing work of His grace and His tactics are to help us make our daily choices through the filter of His grace in our lives.

It's the way God runs His family. If it works for Him, there's a real good chance it will work for your family and your church's family ministry.

ENDNOTES

[1]Much has been written about the "Starbucks experience." And most people are aware of the period in their corporate history when Starbucks lost its way. Starbucks CEO, Howard Schultz, unpacked this corporate crisis in his telling and transparent book, *Onward*. There is much that pastors and parents can gain from the lessons

Starbucks learned the hard way. In the process of their success, they moved away from the distinctives that made them great in the first place. For churches and families it's the equivalent of the point we're making in this chapter. They had lost their commitment to the quality of their product and the sense of "relationship" with their customer. Families and churches, busy with the issues of the Christian's agenda can easily forget that without genuine loving relationships, it doesn't matter how good, accurate, or urgent our message is. Jesus didn't separate His love for people from His message to the people. We can't either.

[2]Kenneth Boa, *Conformed to His Image: Biblical and Practical Approaches to Spiritual Formation* (Grand Rapids: Zondervan, 2001), p. 71. Bracketed words added.

[3]Lawrence O. Richards. *Expository Dictionary of Bible Words.* Zondervan Publishing House: Grand Rapids. Pp. 319-320.

CHAPTER 4

THE PLACE OF GRACE

F ollow me to a church for a minute:

- † The address—prominent.
- † The architecture—inviting.
- † The facility—state-of-the-art.
- † The pastor—pedigreed.
- † The greeters—warm.
- † The bulletin—four-color.
- † The seats—cushioned.
- † The flowers—fresh.
- † The musicians—this side of professional.
- † The song selection—God-focused.
- † The video set-up—gripping.
- † The sermon—theologically orthodox, biblically layered, and personally inspiring.

Meanwhile you dropped your kids off at departments where the professionals on staff are culturally savvy. The rooms are age-appropriately decorated. The teachers are prepared. The curriculum is biblically strong. The worship is spirited.

This is a church working overtime *to get* everything right.

Now join me as we follow home one of their committed families:

- ✝ The house—comfortable.
- ✝ The finances—adequate.
- ✝ The parents—conscientious.
- ✝ The children—respectful.
- ✝ The worldview—Christian.
- ✝ Nobility—prominent.
- ✝ Obedience—expected.
- ✝ The Bible—the standard.
- ✝ Prayer—daily.
- ✝ Education—thorough.
- ✝ Hard work—typical.
- ✝ Traditions—honored.
- ✝ Individual interests—encouraged.
- ✝ A positive commitment to church—assumed.

This is a family working overtime *to do* everything right.

The church tried to think of everything when it came to carrying out the work of the ministry, and the parents tried to do the same. There's only one thing missing in both this church and this home:

They don't have a heating and air conditioning system.

When you're trying to worship or listen to the sermon, the room is 35° F in the winter and 102° F in the summer. It's the same way in this home as the parents and family members try to conscientiously live out their Christian convictions. Regardless of how much they try, it's extremely difficult for the people within this church and this home to respond well to all of the spiritual efforts being done on their behalf. The contrary atmosphere has negated much of the right actions.

Now obviously, no physical structure of a modern-day church

or family dwelling would be built without a heating and air conditioning system. But from a spiritual point of view, that's exactly what's going on in many churches and homes. They've kept the everyday priority of God's transforming work of grace out of the primary blueprints for *how* they do what they are doing spiritually. Activities, accomplishments, and assumptions can be simply busy work without the context of relationship in a family or church. It's God's grace lived out that creates the kind of atmosphere where His truth can be appreciated and appropriated.

This isn't a putdown; it's just an observation.

THE PLACE OF GRACE

God's grace is supposed to be the spiritual climate control system of the church and Christian family relationships—whether we want to acknowledge it or not. It's what Jesus used to define the relationships within His team of disciples. It's what He brought to the forefront with the people He encountered in His public ministry.

God's transforming work of grace is the factor that most determines the ambience between people's hearts. It's the power and presence of God's grace working through the lives of the people running a church or a family that inclines the folks on the receiving end of their efforts toward the greater message of the gospel and a personal desire to bring the best out of each other.

Grace is simply God's love showing itself in relational determination.

Think about this for a minute. When you go into a church or a home, you can't see the air quality but you can sense it. Your physical system immediately records if there's something wrong with the environment. If a person is freezing or burning up, it's very difficult for him or her to appreciate whatever else might be going on—even if it's something being done (said, taught) for his or her greater good.

It's easy for churches and families to quantify their beliefs, doctrines, and biblical priorities. Grace isn't something that is measured the same way. It's more *experienced* through the *quality* of our love and commitment to each other. Biblical orthodoxy is a lot about what we know. Grace is more about how we come across (or what we're known for). A biblically focused church and family is often understood as something we do. A grace-based church and family is most often understood as something we are.

IT WORKS FOR GOD

God is a God of relationship. Our Trinitarian understanding of God is vital to grasping the priority of God's grace when it comes to how we operate within our churches and families. God is One. If this were our singular understanding of Him, it would be easy to camp on the features of His all-encompassing power and greatness as our Creator and His wrath as the Righteous Judge. But although God is One—and those features I just mentioned about Him are indeed true—He exists in three persons. Those persons have *always* existed in a state of outwardly focused love for each other. God loves the Son, the Son loves the Spirit, the Spirit loves the Father, the Father loves the Spirit, the Son loves the Father. You get the idea. Outwardly active love has always been one of the defining features of God's relationship within His divine nature.

And so, although hard to grasp when viewed through human eyes, it made perfect sense to God to want to show His love through the power of His grace to the sinful human race that had turned their back on Him. The single greatest act of divine love was when our Triune God worked in perfect concert to redeem sinful humanity through the sacrifice of Jesus on the cross for our sins. Through His death, burial, and resurrection, He made it possible for individual people like you and me to have a pathway straight to His redemptive heart.

Can I get a witness?

No one who has gained a saving relationship with God through Jesus questions the reality of God's grace. We know full well why "Amazing Grace" is the most universally recognized hymn in the world. Anyone whom Jesus has saved from his or her sins is categorically certain he or she has received something undeserved. We were doomed and needed a Savior. God's grace supplied us with one, personally.

MISGUIDED THINKING

The problem many, many Christians have is that we "get" grace if we're talking about "saving" grace. But we have a bad habit of leaving that saving grace right where we found it at the foot of the cross and then going right back on a performance basis with God in our Christian walk.

We assume there is now a *behavioral expectation* on us that will determine the quality and quantity of God's on-going love toward us.

Stop a minute. Perhaps go back and read that previous sentence again—and again if you need to—until its point hits home. We actually proceed in our Christian lives under the false assumption that the quality or the quantity of God's on-going love is dependent on our behavior. When I read that statement I can almost hear God saying something like, "Are you kidding me? You actually think My love is being held back from you? That I'm somehow holding out on you until I get the kind of behavior from you I'm expecting in return for all that I did for you on cross? Are you serious? I *can't* give you *more* of My love because I'm *always* giving you *all* of it! If your behavior had anything to do with whether or not you'd receive My love, trust me, you wouldn't get anything from Me! I don't love you because of how you act or live your life. I love you period! I love you because that is my intrinsic divine nature. I enjoy loving you!" God can't and won't love us more based on our behavior. That's not how His love works.

We may never say it out loud, but there develops in many followers of Jesus this subtle sense that our primary purpose is to impress God and appease Him by obeying Him; that somehow, God's kindness, blessings, and watch-care are contingent on our day-to-day behavior. Obedience is a wonderful and logical response to the love of God on our behalf, but it can become a toxic feature of our relationship with Him if we're obeying God for all the wrong reasons—biblically flawed reasons.

So, the "goodness" that should be more the *natural* outgrowth of a heart in love with God instead becomes more of our focus and preoccupation—a *quid pro quo* arrangement with God. It becomes our spiritual duty and obligation. This type of arrangement promotes fear and creates worry in the believer. Guilt and shame can dominate the back rooms of our thinking as we consider the many ways we fall short of God's expectations. This inclines us to operate more masked and guarded around other Christians, uncomfortable with letting them get too close to us lest they see us for what we really are—spiritual failures walking around on feet of clay. Our need to measure up breeds judgmental spirits toward both believers and unbelievers that fall short in their own lives. We're predisposed to create a church environment that panders to people who are more in line with our behavioral checklist. Next thing you know we're creating all kinds of noble, but man-made, systems to prop up our nice Christian behavior—an outside-in management plan for our spiritual deportment that takes the place of the work of God the Holy Spirit. Here comes the pride, followed by our self-righteousness.

This is what happens when we leave the grace that saved

us at the foot of the cross. If anything, this is a recipe for angry evangelicalism, spiritual elitism, and arrogant dogmatism. And the leaders of any church or family can find themselves falling into these traps even though they are committed to some of the finest features of evangelical beliefs: a clear teaching of the truth of God, a priority on the authority of the Scripture, orthodox doctrine, strong apologetics, a biblical worldview, God-focused worship, worldwide evangelism, and relief for the downtrodden. These are all wonderful features of our faith, but for them to stay pure they must always be framed, defined, and tempered with the power and presence of God's transforming *grace*.

A QUEST FOR A THEOLOGY OF FAMILY

When my wife, Darcy, and I knew we were going to have our first child, we did what a lot of young Christian couples do when they're going to have a baby: We read the different Christian books available. Although some of them were very helpful, for the most part, we were disappointed in what we found. We weren't disappointed because we were somehow above the writers spiritually—not by a long shot. We were disappointed because we desperately wanted to do this parenting thing right and were taken aback at the presuppositions (philosophy) that seemed to frame so many of the works we read.

We were surprised at how many came from a fear-based parenting perspective. Their focus slipped back and forth between the sinister nature of the enemies of darkness and the corrupted world system that surrounded us. Add to that equation our children's predilection towards folly and stupidity and you've got the philosophical starting point for a fear-based plan for parenting. Their strategy was sin management with tactics that involved a lot of evangelical behavioral modification.

Sorry, but we weren't interested in that kind of a plan for

parenting. For one thing, it was fueled by fear and focused on the threats facing us. We didn't question the legitimacy of all of their concerns: There is a nasty power working against us that wants to eat us and our kids for dinner; our culture *is* corrupted; and we give birth to kids who, left to their own devices, will make utter fools of themselves. But Darcy and I had put our faith in a God who is bigger than all of those challenges. We wanted a parenting plan that was fueled by God's love and focused on God's power.

The other books we read dialed in heavily on discipline. Although discipline and correction of children is clearly part of the job of a parent, we were hoping that being parents would be a bit more enjoyable than trying to outwit our kids while standing on their air hoses. On top of all of this, there was no overarching theology that anyone put forth that helped frame our roles and goals as parents. There were some great passages of Scripture that gave good "strategic" and "tactical" advice on raising kids, passages like Deuteronomy 6:4-9, Ephesians 6:1-4, and Colossians 3:20-21; but they didn't make up a theology or spiritual context for parenting.

Yet we both felt certain that God wouldn't create a parent/child arrangement and put so much priority for human outcome on that arrangement and not give us a clear plan to follow. It's just not like Him to do that. So we prayed like mad and began our search of the Scriptures for this "theology of family."

Then we had one of those "Aha!" moments. It was actually a rather simple observation that should go without saying. "Wait a minute, God, You're a parent. You're parenting us. We're Your children. I wonder if we could take what You're doing with us, quantify it, and then put handles on it in such a way that we could use it as our method of raising our kids?"

When we made that observation and asked that question, the theology of family suddenly materialized center stage in our Bibles. It had been there all along, from cover to cover. God is a God of grace. When it comes to His relationship with us, He both connects to us and maintains that connection through the sweaty hard work of His grace in our lives. Truth, orthodox doctrine, Scripture memorization, apologetics, biblical worldview, obedience, etc. were all still a part of our parenting plan. But they had to always exist and process in concert with God's heart of grace. It was God's *grace* that would create the comfortable room temperature atmosphere between our children and us. It was God's *grace* that would create the heart connection with our children that would enhance all of the other biblical and spiritual things we were trying to transfer to them.

WHY GRACE CREEPS OUT SOME PEOPLE

Let's deal with the obvious. For some hard-to-understand reason, grace makes a lot of church leaders nervous. It makes a lot of parents nervous. When a person like me comes along and suggests that God's grace should be the starting point of our theology/ philosophy of family, the framework of its strategy and the punch line of its tactics, sometimes people just go nuts!

Why is that?

I've been at this a while and can distill the answer to that question down to three primary reasons.

REASON 1: Some parents and church leaders get nervous when we talk about making grace the DNA of their family relationships and family ministry because they mistake biblical grace for "always being nice" or "giving people license" or "being a pushover." Question: Is God primarily nice? Does God jettison His rulebook with the human race when we enter into a relationship with Him through His grace? Is God a pushover? No, no, and no. There are a lot of folks who drop the grace bomb when they're in trouble as a way to manipulate you to circumvent the consequences for their folly. That's not grace. That's mercy. So, some parent may want to reject grace as a framework for family relationships, but they do that based on a *faulty* understanding of God's grace. God isn't a pushover who lets the people He loves get away with stupid stuff. Darcy and I wanted to have a grace-based home, but that never stopped us from still being authoritative parents that raised our children within clear biblical boundaries.

REASON 2: Some feel that giving grace the prominent position in defining their relationship with their family members relegates God's truth to a benign position. I hear it all the time, "Yea, Tim, but what about truth?" When people throw that question at me I instantly know something about them that they don't know about themselves—something they would never admit. Namely, they don't "get" grace. Oh, they get the *saving* nature of grace all right, but they don't see the ongoing and transforming role of it. If they did, they'd never ask such a clueless and unbiblical question.

Speaking of questions, let me ask you a couple. First question: Is God dealing with us in grace? Second question: Does He deny His truth or relegate it to an inferior position in the bigger picture of His relationship with us? Yes to the first and no to the second.

John 1:14 says, "The Word [Jesus] became flesh and made his dwelling among us. We have seen his glory, the glory of the one and only Son, who came from the Father, full of grace and truth" (brackets added). *Full* of grace and *full* of *truth*. It wasn't a 50/50 split or a 75/25 split. It was a 100/100. A parent can clearly emulate Christ in dealing with their children in the power of His grace while still holding to all of the empirical and practical truth that the Bible teaches about God. In fact, that's the *only* way you can do it! Darcy and I wanted to have a grace-based home, but that never limited us from still teaching our kids the whole council of God's truth. It enhanced it.

Face it, it's a proven *fact* that people can be totally committed to teaching and upholding the letter of the Word of God (truth) and miss the whole point of the gracious heart of God (grace).

There was an extreme example of this in the gospel accounts: the Pharisees. They harangued Jesus about His gracious treatment of people all the time. And they used the "truth" of the Scriptures and their misguided interpretations and applications of it as their legal defense for hammering Him. They were the experts in the Law. They definitely should have known better. And they were the only people that Jesus got visibly, verbally, and physically angry with.

Listen, you can have a truth-based family ministry at church and a truth-based configuration in the home without having any grace in place. The Pharisees and their ilk did it all the time. Maybe that's why Paul reminded us that "knowledge puffs up while love builds up."[1] Maybe that's why Peter signed his letters with the statement, "But grow in the grace <u>and</u> knowledge of our Lord and Savior Jesus Christ."[2] Can you have a grace-based family ministry at church and a grace-based family configuration in the home without prioritizing God's truth? The answer is a resounding NO! Not if we're talking about *biblical* grace. It CAN'T happen. Can you have a truth-based system and not have grace? Absolutely! Truth-based systems are all about the priority of Scripture, Bible knowledge, Christian doctrine, apologetical arguments, and theology. But they can be, and often are, transferred without God's grace attached.

I guess you can see why the "truth" question makes me sad.

REASON 3: Some people get nervous about letting grace define their relationships because they know the only way to accomplish such is through trusting God with your life . . . moment by moment, day by day. It's so much easier to define your relationships through authority, rules, consequences, truth, biblical knowledge, and Christian behavioral checklists.

THE ELEPHANT IN THE ROOM

Folks, there's an elephant in the room. A long time ago I learned a great rule for life: If there's an elephant in the room, for heaven's sake, someone introduce him. Friend, there's a lot of family ministry and Christian parenting going on that contradicts the message its trying to send to the people involved. I see a lot of emphasis placed on spiritual performance, behavioral report carding, creating biblical elitism, guilting people who struggle, shaming people who fall, nagging people who are slow to buy in, marginalizing people who question, and rejecting people who refuse to toe the line.

My question: *Is that how God treats us?*

Also, there are times when what's happening behind the scenes in the dynamics between professional staff and/or volunteers at church is a walking, breathing contradiction to God's heart of grace. The same thing can happen at home between parents. Bickering Christians demean the faith. Trust me, the kids figure this out. It has a negating effect on all of the legitimate things the church and the parents are trying to transfer to them. That's why we not only need to start from a position of God's grace, but also function in its power.

DEFINING GRACE-BASED RELATIONSHIPS

There is good news, though! The solution to the challenges that face families and family ministries is not complicated or out of reach. In fact, like so many of God's solutions to our needs, it's surprisingly simple. A grace-based family ministry and a grace-based family parenting relationship can be summarized in one sentence:

Treating others the way God treats us.

ENDNOTES

[1] 1 Corinthians 8:1.

[2] 2 Peter 3:18, Underline added for emphasis.

CHAPTER 5

PAPER NAPKIN FAMILY MINISTRY

Do you like diners? 'Cause I'd like to take you to one. Any diner in general will do. As long as it has booths with chrome trimmed Formica tables, waitresses that chew gum, awesome coffee, and a great selection of pies, it'll work for what I have in mind.

We're going to take someone with us. Let's take either a person from a church that has responsibility for what happens with families (the pastor, the family pastor, the youth pastor) or let's take a parent. You sit next to me across from him or her. After we've all ordered our pie, here's what I'd like to do. I'm going to pull one of these nice paper napkins out of the dispenser here, take my ball point pen out of my pocket, and slide them both over to this church leader or parent. This is why I wanted a diner for this exercise. Nice restaurants frown on writing on their cloth napkins.

I want this leader or parent to please lay out for you and me their overarching plan for raising his or her kids and transferring a heart of faith to the children in his or her church.

Suppose the person clicks the pen into a writing position and without hesitation writes four key points across the top of the napkin:

PRAYER • BIBLE • CHURCH • CHRISTIAN LIVING

Then he or she takes them one at a time:

PRAYER

† I'll pray for my kids everyday—especially that they come to know Jesus.

† I'll teach them to pray.

† (If he or she is the parent) I'll pray with them at night before they go to sleep.

† I'll show them how to keep a prayer journal.

† We'll keep track of prayers answered to show them how powerful prayer truly is.

BIBLE

† I'll make sure they learn all of the main stories of the Bible.

† I'll make sure they know the orthodox doctrines on the main issues.

† I'll show them how good theology binds everything together.

† I'll encourage them to read their Bible regularly.

† I'll help them memorize Scripture.

† I'll teach them the most logical arguments to use when dealing with someone's protest towards the Bible.

† I'll help them see their world through a biblical lens.

† (Parent) I'll read and discuss the Bible with them several times a week through devotions.

CHURCH

- † I'll participate with them at church.
- † I'll teach them the value of faithful attendance.
- † I'll build into them a priority for worshiping God.
- † I'll teach them the importance of giving financially to the church.
- † I'll teach them the value of serving by having them volunteer in the children's department, on a worship team, parking cars, greeting people, and/or cleaning up afterwards.

CHRISTIAN LIVING

- † I'll teach them the value of having good Christian friends.
- † I'll teach them the value of being a good Christian friend.
- † I'll warn them of the various traps within their culture.
- † I'll teach them how to represent Jesus to others who don't know Him.
- † (Parent) I'll discipline and correct them when they stray off course.

Okay. I think that just about fills up the napkin—front and back, writing small, and opening it up to write on the inside.

Now, let's study this person's overarching plan (philosophy, strategy, or tactics) he or she is using to develop kids who will carry on a passionate legacy of faith in Christ. What do you think? At the outset, I have to say that I truly like all of the things I'm seeing. There are always other things we'd like to add to that list if it were ours to tamper with; but we only have a single napkin. Besides, if we can't distill our "overarching plan" down to a single napkin, most likely, we don't have one.

At first glance, what I'm seeing on this napkin is a list of great dimensions of faith I'd like my kids to know and have going for them when they head into adulthood. These are all good things.

If this is the "plan" we have for transferring a passionate heart for Jesus into our kids, there are four groups of people who will really like it: fear-based parents, sin managers, image controllers, and churches that grade Christian maturity on spiritual performance.

Question: Do you know anyone who has been raised in this kind of environment that grew up not wanting to have anything to do with God? I do. Tons of them. Yet, the items on this list are the anchor tenants of most conscientious family ministries and Christian homes.

Does that mean there's something wrong with the things on this list?

Of course not!

What it means is this isn't an overarching plan we can assume has a high probability of developing kids who will carry on a passionate legacy of faith in Christ. It's a great outline for a curriculum for a church, family, or Christian school to pass on great biblical information and spiritual disciplines to a child. But it's no philosophical, strategic, or tactical plan for parenting or for family ministry.

As it stands, its chance of being transformational has little or nothing to do with any of the items on the list. That's because it's about concepts, information, and behavior. It does not frame any kind of relationship between the persons on the giving or receiving ends of the plan. We must never forget that the core of the gospel is a love *relationship* and heart *connection* that has the power to transform sinners into saints. Moving our children from childhood to a passionate Jesus follower is going to require a lot more than a list of great Christian precepts.

LET'S TRY AGAIN

Let's say the person (parent or church leader) takes the napkin and writes some very different words at the top:

TIME • FUN • COACHING

They elaborate. "In our church (or family), we spell love: T·I·M·E. We want to make sure children don't feel like they are fitting into gaps in our schedule but rather our schedule is designed around them. Another way of saying this is we want to give them a lot of personal focus. This would be seen in the kind of room we provide them at home (or church), the amenities we surround their life with, and the budget we set aside for their unique interests. We want them to know they are not only on our minds, but also a key part of our agenda."

"We want to make getting to know God fun. This would be reflected in our programming at church, the kind of Christian professionals we provide; great camping experiences; exciting mission options with great destinations; and a lot of commitment within their church experiences for laughter, skits, and crazy competitions. At home, we want to use a lot of fun videos, games, and books to help transfer the vital information we want them to know about Jesus." "Kids need to know we care. They need to know that we know what they're up against. We'll be there as coaches in their life. Whether we coach them as parents or church leaders, we want them to know that we're there for them to set a great example and voice encouraging words as they take on life. We'll do our best to use biblical teaching and spiritual exercises to groom them for real life."

Okay, once again, nice job! I like so much of what I'm hearing.

It's hard to fault a plan that presents such judicious gifts to a child as time, fun, and coaching. Childhood goes better with all of these. Parents and churches that are deliberate about these things are going to naturally find kids more at ease around them. It definitely puts a favorable light on the greater issues a church is supposed to address.

Yet, without a clear *context* for transferring specific biblical truth to children, kids raised in this kind of family or church environment might feel loved and even led, but not necessarily prepared to carry on their spiritual legacy.

If you took the priorities of the first plan and merged it with the qualities of the second plan, you'd have an extremely nice try. The first plan was more tactical in nature (transferring vital spiritual information). This second plan is more strategic (creating a favorable ambiance that naturally relates to a young person's needs). Most conscientious churches try to do a combination of these two.

Both of these represent programs and concepts that have great value, but seem to be incomplete. The first is more of a Bible Institute approach of transferring a spiritual legacy and the second works more off of a Christian Resort approach. There's clearly a place for both in the Christian journey, but if either approach wants to be effective, they need to have something more defining the efforts than great biblical information and cool activities.

THE HONEST APPROACH

Suppose the parent or church leader picks up the clean, white paper napkin, stares at it for a few moments, and then writes something like this:

No Clue—I'm just going to love them like mad, pray for them like mad, and hope for the best.

Actually, this honest approach isn't that bad either. Most parents (and a lot of churches) might find this response far more in line with their personal reality. And there's no doubt that God has done a lot of great things in young people's lives through the love, prayers, and hopes of the people trying to raise them.

But we can all see the gaps in this approach. It's accidental rather than deliberate. That wouldn't be so bad if Satan just did an occasional drive-by on our kids. But he relentlessly carpet-bombs them day in and day out. Add to that the cultural competition they face when it comes to their spiritual values and their internal battle with selfishness and you can see how this approach would have a high failure rate.

JOURNEYS

Earlier, I mentioned my wife, Darcy, and I found ourselves facing this very dilemma when it came to raising our kids. What was our overarching plan going to be? I even had years as a youth pastor under my belt when we brought our first child home from the hospital. But because of the conventional way that Christian parents and Christian churches have approached this challenge, we found ourselves, just like everyone else, inclined to either put the emphasis on transferring the right information or trying our best to make the journey as enjoyable and painless as possible.

Parenting required more than this. Our kids needed more than this. God deserved better than this.

That's what put us on a deliberate journey to find a more intentional, comprehensive plan. This quest took us back to the foot of the cross. It was from that vantage point that we were able to reclaim the role of the amazing grace we had originally found there in salvation—a grace that was longing to frame the relationships God had called us to with our children. God's role as a parent in our lives gave us all we needed to recreate an effective, overarching philosophy, strategy, and tactics for transferring a passionate love for Him to our kids.

A NAPKIN COVERED WITH GOD'S GRACE

With this in mind, let's take a blank napkin out of the dispenser, and may I humbly offer up for your review one other option? Please note that I would draw out the EXACT SAME thing whether I was drawing it as the plan for our family or the family ministry at our church. Incidentally, if you change the target of the plan (from kids to whomever) this is the EXACT SAME plan I'd draw out for my marriage, friendships, our church in general, or any of the departments of our church in particular. I'd use the exact same plan if I was drawing out a grace-based napkin plan for a company too.

If someone slid a paper napkin to me and asked me to unpack a philosophy, strategy, and tactics for transferring a passionate heart for Jesus to the next generation, I'd write out something like this:

I want to connect to the heart of my child in such a way that I condition them to have a tender heart for God.

I'll do this through the power of God's grace!

Grace-based relationships (within family or ministry) is simply treating each other the way God treats us.

(Then I'd draw a house with these words on it)

(I'd flip the napkin over and fill in the finer points of these four dimensions of God's grace.)

By making God's grace the philosophical starting point of everything we do, we guarantee that whatever is done will be done within an authentic connection to our kids' heart. Just step back for a second and look at how God lovingly deals with us:

† He sees our truest needs (inner needs)

† He knows our deepest longings (freedom)

† He understands our greatest challenges (character)

† He envisions our highest potential (true greatness)

Jesus did all of these things as He encountered people throughout His three years of public ministry (and probably every year leading up to it seeing how he was *full* of grace and truth[1]). You can see this in:

† The renaming of Cephas to Peter[2]

† His night visit with Nicodemus[3]

† His attitude towards the pushy children that wanted to get close to Him[4]

† The determined men who dropped their crippled friend through a hole they'd made in a roof[5]

† Zaccheus[6]

† The woman caught in adultery[7]

† The rich young ruler[8]

† His mother[9]

† The Samaritan woman[10]

† The guy who had been blind from birth[11]

† His friends Mary, Martha, and their brother Lazarus[12]

† The disciples as a group and individually

† The hungry people on the side of the hill[13]

† The crazy man in the tombs[14]

† Jairus and his daughter[15]

† The thief on the cross[16]

† The conversion of Paul[17] (to name a few)

What Jesus was doing in every one of these encounters was working from the power of His grace to make a heart connection to these people that put them in the best position to accept His truth and respond to His call.

And then there was Calvary. In six raw hours of bitter suffering, our *needs, longings, challenges,* and *potential* were all satisfied in this singular act of grace. Jesus went to the cross so the relationship between God and humanity, that had been severed by sin, could be restored once and for all.

When God's grace is the philosophical starting point of our family ministry at home and at church, it not only assumes a position of love for them, but it must be steered by the gospel. It is family, church, and Bible training that is completely saturated with God's gracious and loving heart. It's parent/child and church/family dynamics that are defined by God's grace at the relational level. God's grace creates a relationship that inclines a people's heart toward the good news, gives credibility to the truth we want to embed in their hearts, and gives passion to the influence God wants them to have in the lives of the people they touch.

† You can't sustain this without being a person who prays.

† You can't sustain this without being a person who has a regular relationship with God through His Word.

† You can't sustain this and stay ignorant about orthodox doctrine.

† You can't sustain this without being broken and humble before God.

† You can't sustain this on your own steam.

† You can't sustain this without the power and presence of God holding the high ground in your heart.

Grace determines everything—the starting point, the finish line, and everything in between. It keeps the process in balance. And it keeps our human shortcomings in check. When homes and churches embrace God's grace together, the dance happens.

ENDNOTES

[1]John 1:14.

[2]John 1:35-42.

[3]John 3:1-21.

[4]Matthew 19:13-14.

[5]Luke 5:17-26.

[6]Luke 19:1-9.

[7]John 8:1-11.

[8]Mark 10:17-31.

[9]John 2:1-11; 19:25-26.

[10]John 4:1-42.

[11]John 9.

[12]Luke 10:38-42; John 11:1-45.

[13]John 6:1-15.

[14]Luke 8:26-38.

[15]Luke 8:40-56.

[16]Matthew 27:44; Luke 23:39-43.

[17]Acts 9:1-19.

CHAPTER 6

GRACE-BASED FAMILIES; GRACE-BASED FAMILY MINISTRIES

S ince my youth, God, you have taught me, and to this day I declare your marvelous deeds. Even when I am old and gray, do not forsake me, my God, till I declare your power to the next generation, your mighty acts to all who are to come" (Psalm 71:17–18).

God has done something marvelous for us. In turn, through the power of His grace, we get to pass on a legacy of His power and might to the next generation. As Neil Postman said, "Children are the living messages we send to a time we will not see."[1] They can be a breathing, thinking, and active message of the powerful and loving God we serve *if* we handle our role as their parents and leaders properly.

This concept of passing down a legacy sounds so *inspiring*. But it sure takes on a mind of its own when you try to implement it. It's tempting to think the psalmist had someone else in mind besides you or me when it comes to leaving this powerful spiritual legacy—someone who came from a better family of origin, someone with a higher relational and biblical IQ, a nuclear family type that fits the cliché but is more the exception than the rule.

What about those parents who come to church with heavy hearts and hopes running thin? What's their chance of leaving this kind of legacy? It might be the folks with a son who can't figure out how to concentrate in school or their nice Christian daughter who has suddenly gone Goth (or whatever is in vogue at the time). Sometimes it's just an overriding ache they bring because the job of being a mother or father is so huge and they simply don't know what they're supposed to be doing—especially if they're doing it solo. And then there are those very dangerous hurts that bring the parents searching for answers from the family ministry at church, like the full-blown prodigal with his ugly insults, self-destructive habits, and gigantic chip on his shoulder; or the pregnant teenaged daughter; or her sister who's stopped eating.

Parenting is one of the most profound and influential tasks that any adult will undertake. A mother and father hold a significant part of the future in their arms when they bring that son or daughter home. To that child, these parents will be the greatest source of either goodness or harm of any other person in his or her life. The sheer weight of the responsibility is enough to make most parents wish they had chosen to raise Labradors instead.

Besides holding part of the future in their arms, parents also hold a piece of eternity. So much of what they do will play a significant role in the kind of relationship that son or daughter will ultimately develop with God.

And so families come looking for answers, looking for relief, looking for hope.

LEAVING LEGACIES THAT NEVER DIE

There are some parents who come to church with a fairly strong heart-connection to their children. They are true allies and assets to what the church's family ministry is trying to accomplish. But there are too many parents who have lost that heart connection or never had it in the first place. They are confused, frustrated, discouraged, and angry. They're also scared. They're afraid of what might happen to their child if things don't improve. Some are also afraid that once the leaders at church start sorting out the pieces of their family puzzle, they might figure out that it's them—the mother or father—that's the biggest part of the problem.

Effective family ministry isn't about blame or guilt; it's about *hope*. When it comes to trying to raise kids without having a clue what we're doing spiritually, the line of parents stretches as far as the eye can see. I've stood in the line at times, and so have you. Church leaders need to be able to assure these desperate and heavy-hearted parents that there is something substantive and time-tested that can be done to help them bridge the vast divide between them and their child. But we need to make sure that it's not just some advice we hand from a curriculum that bandages the present problem but does little to frame a bigger and more comprehensive solution. Whatever we do needs to be a direct extension of God's love working from our heart.

Fortunately, not all of the families showing up at church are on spiritual life-support. And even those that are, have more going for them than they think. Most parents feel inadequate and overwhelmed when they step back and take an honest assessment of what they're up against. It's standard operating procedure to second-guess oneself when it comes to passing a passionate faith from one generation to the next.

But God has given all of us everything we need to leave the Psalm 71-kind-of legacy. He's given us His grace. It's a grace that is sufficient; a grace that turns into a power that God uses to perfect us in the midst of our weaknesses.[2] Grace is a relational manifestation of God's love. It's the secret weapon for parents and family ministers who want to embed a living faith into the hearts of their children. As such it gives us the capacity to love our children deeply. The good news is *that* kind of love covers a multitude of our human shortcomings and relational mistakes.[3] God always meant for the grace that saved us to also be the grace that defines our relationships with the people surrounding us.

When domestic churches and local churches allow God's grace to define their culture, amazing things happen. Spiritual stock values rise. Relationships deepen. Trust spikes. Fears dissipate. Suspicions lose traction. Biblical teaching penetrates deeper. Leaders (parents) enjoy greater confidence from the people they're called to influence. Forgiveness assumes the high ground. Joy shows up and decides to stay. Discipline and correction are more gently applied and more readily accepted. Peace settles within hearts. And, humility leads the way.

Everything I just listed is what happens when we let God's truth guide us and let His grace define us and transform us. When God's grace permeates a home or church, all of the other noble, biblical, and spiritual efforts thrive. Even better, the authentic presence of God's transforming grace compensates for the limited biblical sophistication part of most people's profiles in the younger years of their adult life. If grace doesn't permeate homes and churches, good efforts languish. And rightfully so. Why should we expect people to respond positively to spiritual efforts that operate in isolation from the very grace required to have a relationship with God in the first place?

God's grace enables parents and preachers to leave legacies that never die. With all of this as preamble, let's unpack the grace-based philosophy, strategy, and tactics we introduced on a paper napkin in the last chapter. It's grace that God can use to pass on a passionate legacy of faith in Christ to our children and grandchildren.

HIS GRACE IS ALL YOU NEED

Grace is a game-changer. Grace-based parenting and grace-based family ministry is simply treating the people in your (church) family the way God treats the people in His. It's treating your children the way He treats His. If we want to produce a next generation who love God, live for Him, and make an impact in their world, God's grace is the perfect vehicle to make this happen.

Grace-based parenting and family ministry is the combination of four basic extensions of the grace God extends to us. Whether it's to our children or our congregation:

1. We need to meet their driving inner needs.
2. We need to extend to them the same freedoms God gives to us.
3. We need to build them from the inside out with character.
4. We need to aim them at a future of "true" greatness.

The house illustration from the last chapter captures these four powerful extensions of God's gracious heart:

Parenting.FamilyMatters.net   Copyright©TimKimmel2010

Let's break the four dimensions of grace-based parenting (ministry) into their individual component parts starting at the bottom of the house diagram and working our way up.

Dimension 1: Meeting their three driving inner needs.

All children are born with three gnawing and driving needs in their heart. It is to the parent that God has given the primary job of meeting these needs. Here's the problem: most parents couldn't tell you what these needs are if their life depended on it. That's not a put-down. How could the typical parent know what these three inner needs are if someone didn't tell them? Hopefully from here on out we can change this.

Sadly, there is one person who not only knows exactly what these three needs are, but also appeals to them constantly—with counterfeits. His name is Satan. If you want to see him appealing to these in the Bible, just study how he dials in on them in his successful temptation of Eve in Genesis 3. You see him go after these same three needs in his failed effort at tempting Jesus in Matthew 4. It's difficult for parents or family ministries to consistently meet needs in children when those needs aren't even on their radar let alone a part of their daily focus. Since Satan never makes a move on a person without appealing to one or a combination of these needs . . . *and* since God's grace consistently works to fill them in us, it makes sense to know what they are and turn every word or action that comes from us into an opportunity to meet them in legitimate ways.

Inner Need Number 1: All children have a driving inner need for **security**. When it is met, it gives them a confidence that they are deeply *loved*. Our job, therefore, as parents and church leaders, is to use every contact with our children as an opportunity to instill a **secure love** into their hearts. We do this by:

 † Accepting them the way God made them, with their body type, IQ, mannerisms, etc.

† Making sure our homes and churches are loving and honoring environments.

† Being demonstrative to them and showing affection.

Inner Need Number 2: All children have a driving inner need for **significance**. When it is met, it gives them a confidence that they have a greater *purpose* in life. Our job, therefore, as parents and church leaders, is to use every contact with our children as an opportunity to instill a **significant purpose** into their hearts. We do this by:

† Consistently affirming them.

† Giving them individual attention and focus.

† Admonishing, correcting, and disciplining them.

Inner Need Number 3: All children have a driving inner need for **strength**. When it is met, it gives them a confidence that they have *hope* with which to face each day. Our job, therefore, as parents and church leaders, is to use every contact with our children as an opportunity to instill a ***strong hope*** into their hearts. We do this by:

† Working overtime to recognize their God-given abilities and helping develop them.

† Encouraging them to live a life of adventure where they are forced to trust God.

† Turning their years under our care into a series of positive accomplishments.

God's grace consistently meets our needs for a secure love, a significant purpose, and a strong hope. When it comes to grace-based homes and grace-based churches, it goes without saying that we should use every word that comes out of our mouths and every action we have towards our kids to do the same.

Dimension 2: Setting hearts free.

Freedom isn't the license to do whatever we want but the responsibility to do what we should—things best for us and for the people we love.

In the beginning of God's story of His relationship with humanity in Genesis 2:16, you can see that He designed us to have a sense of personal freedom within moral boundaries. "And the LORD God commanded the man, 'You are free to eat from any tree in the garden'" (Genesis 2:16). The psalmist reinforces this unique relationship with God when he states, "I will walk about in freedom, for I have sought out your precepts" (Psalm 119:45). Jesus said, "So, if the Son sets you free, you will be free indeed" (John 8:36). And since we have freely received God's grace, He wants us to freely give it (Matthew 10:8).

With this in mind, there are four wonderful freedoms grace-based parents and family ministries can offer that automatically set a child's heart at ease. These four wonderful gifts draw children's hearts in close to ours. They bring the best out of them. And these four freedoms provide the best atmosphere for meeting the child's driving inner needs for a secure love, a significant purpose, and a strong hope.

First: Grace-based parents and churches give children the freedom to be different.

Good synonyms for "different" are weird, bizarre, strange, goofy, and quirky. We're not talking about the kids doing anything biblically or morally wrong. They're just weird. Grace-based homes and churches have room for these kinds of kids. They celebrate them. So much of these unusual characteristics are actually part of the hardwiring that God placed within them.

Unfortunately, fear-based, sin management, legalistic, and performance-based homes and churches have no room for these kinds of kids. They marginalize them. A standard reaction of parents or churches to a kid's bizarre behavior or quirky mannerisms is to be annoyed or embarrassed. They react by framing their child's behavior as "bad" or "wrong" when in reality it's just "different." Legalistic parents and family ministries often make the mistake of moralizing non-moral behavior (like fashion that is modest, but weird). Or worse, they make a biblical issue out of non-moral and non-biblical behavior. They say things like, "I don't think Jesus would be very pleased with your hair, or music, or clothing" when there's nothing actually morally or biblically wrong with their hair, music, or clothing. They're just *different*. These kinds of attitudes and comments shove wedges between a child's heart and his or her parents (or church leader) and between his and her heart and God. A big part of helping adults on these issues is to move them beyond their reaction to superficial issues and get them more interested in the *heart* of their child—kinda like God is interested in ours.

It's true, that although some children's external appearances may not be wrong per se, they nevertheless might be representing a possible problem within them. Logic says that it's still foolish to react to or critique these external manifestations. It is far better to keep our focus on their heart relationship and let God heal the problem within. Once that's done, the exterior takes care of itself.

Second: Grace-based parents and churches give children the freedom to be vulnerable.

They allow their children's fears, emotions, and inadequacies to come out in the open without those children worrying about these fragile parts of their make-up ever being attacked, marginalized, or used against them. Grace-based parents have a high respect for a child's feelings and fears regardless of how unsophisticated or, at times, irrational they may be. And they have a tender heart toward their children's inadequacies (like learning disorders, the fact that they struggle with certain academic subjects, they're shy, etc.). Often the inadequacies in our children were actually designed into them by God so they could learn, through His grace, to trust Him.

Don't believe me? Just ask Paul. He had a thorn in the flesh that he pleaded with God three times to take away. Each time God said, "No." Then the punch line: "My grace is sufficient for you, for my power is made perfect in weakness" (2 Corinthians 12:9).

A gracious response to our young people's fears or inadequacies is a clear extension of God's heart of grace. Colossians 4:6 says, "Let your conversation be always full of grace, seasoned with salt, so that you may know how to answer everyone."

Third: Grace-based parents and churches give children the freedom to be candid.

These kinds of homes and churches are safe places for children to vocalize the deep issues of their heart—to wrestle out in the open with God, or with us. It might be candor about the doubts they are having regarding God or issues of their faith. It might be candor about temptations or pockets of sin they are struggling with. It might be candor about frustrations or anger they have towards one of their parents. Grace-based homes and churches make it safe and easy for children to articulate these troubling parts of their heart. Obviously, grace doesn't mean the children can voice their frustrations with their parents or leaders at church in a disrespectful way. But they can voice them. Gracious parents and leaders set the example by consistently showing respect when voicing their concerns about a child's wrong actions or flawed thinking. As we're reminded by the writer of Hebrews, "See to it that no one falls short of the grace of God and that no bitter root grows up to cause trouble and defile many" (Hebrews 12:15).

God encourages candor. In Hebrews 4:14ff, we see that Jesus our High Priest was tempted just like we are (although without sin). He knows what we're up against. He knows what it feels like in our skin; what it feels like when life and relationships don't go the way we hoped. He knows why people feel frustrated and let down. Summarizing this connection that God has with our hearts, the writer of Hebrews says, "For we do not have a high priest who is unable to empathize with our weaknesses .... Let us then approach God's throne of grace with confidence, so that we may receive mercy and find grace to help us in our time of need" (Hebrews 4:15–16).

It's amazing how much confidence kids have in our position, authority, and influence when we allow them to vocalize the frustrations they are processing in their heart without lectures, sermons, guilt, or shame coming back at them. It's simply giving them the same freedom God gives us.

Fourth: Grace-based parents and churches give children the freedom to make mistakes.

Performance-based spiritual scorekeepers seem so shocked when kids mess up. They take kid's infractions personally. They're known to display utter disappointment when kids foul up even as young as one year old. And they really have a tough time processing the dumb choices the teenagers have a reputation of making.

Grace-based parents and church leaders aren't the least bit surprised when kids mess up. They're sinners (like their parents and leaders). They were born sinners. It's what they have a sophisticated capacity to do straight out of the shoot.

Parents and leaders aren't surprised that children struggle with lying, passing blame, responding in an unacceptable way to their siblings, or speaking in an inappropriate way to their parents. Nor do they take it personally—even if it's personally directed at them. They just do their best to catch as many of the kids' mistakes and graciously deal with them accordingly. Grace isn't passive towards sin. It clearly upholds the moral and relational guidelines of the Bible and disciplines children when they make mistakes. But it always does it graciously without cultivating shame and with the child's best interest in mind.

Contrary to the rumors of the standard legalist, grace isn't a lower standard; it's a higher holiness. The discipline and corrections of a parent are a key part of transferring God's grace to a child's heart. It says to the child, "I love you too much to let you grow up to be foolish. I love you too much to watch you squander your potential. I'm going to discipline you."

The meeting of the three inner needs and the giving of these four freedoms make up the atmosphere of a grace-based home and grace-based churches. They are that comfortable room temperature in relationships that enable all of our other efforts to be more easily received. They are the same needs we have met and freedoms we have extended to us in our relationship with Christ.

For a deeper study on these first two dimensions of grace-based relationships (inner needs and freedoms) you might want to look more closely at the book entitled (of all things) *Grace Based Parenting*, (Kimmel, Thomas Nelson Publishers) at *shop.familymatters.net*.

Dimension 3: Build character into the inner core of their heart.

The third way God shows His grace is by using His power and presence (through His Spirit and His Word) to build character into our lives. Character is the mettle and grit that empowers kids to face life's challenges with confidence. Character is like the studs, joists, beams, and tie downs in houses that give it strength to take on all of the harsh elements that work it over year after year. In the same way, character is what gracious parents and church leaders build into kids that help them when they're afraid, tempted, lonely, or betrayed.

If you take every character word in the Bible, write them all out on a single (big) sheet of paper (I've done this), you'll find (at least I did) that they fall into six general categories. What you have here is the word that I placed at the top of each column that was the all-encompassing header-type word. I borrowed one word from the English dictionary (poise) because it better captured the words in that column.

When we graciously do the tedious, repetitive work of building these character traits into our kids, we prepare them to appropriate God's power and presence as much more of a rule than an exception.

1. **Faith**—becomes a character trait when what we believe starts making moral choices for us.

2. **Integrity**— is the moral clarity we depend on to do the right thing even when life is holding a gun to our head or when no one would know otherwise.

3. **Poise**—is that moral and relational equilibrium that keeps people balanced, practical, and relevant. God's gracious presence in a person's life helps him or her know when it's time to plant or uproot, tear down or build, weep or laugh, mourn or dance, embrace or refrain, search or give up, keep or throw away, be silent or speak up, love or hate, go to war or make peace

(Ecclesiastes 3:1-8; 7:16-18).

4. **Disciplines**—like the rails beneath a train, the disciplines we build into a young person's life enables him or her to harness all of the many potentials God has built into that child. Train tracks confine a train, but in so doing, empower it to do an enormous amount of good for people and the marketplace. A train that leaves its rails is called a "train wreck." Trains wrecks are a mess. So are the lives of people who don't have disciplines built into the core of their character. Grace-based parents and churches love kids enough to do the hard work of building tracks for their potential.

5. **Endurance**—the world is full of quitters. This gracious character trait trains young people to keep going when everyone else would have long given up (1 Corinthians 9:24-27).

6. **Courage**—I like the way John Wayne said it, "Courage is when you're scared to death, but you saddle up anyway."[4] If disciplines are what we put around our children's strengths in order to harness them, courage is what we wrap around our kid's weaknesses and fears in order to help them move beyond them. Just as God's grace courageously drove Jesus to center stage of time and space to pay the price for our sins on the cross, it can also empower His children to face the giants in their life.

These six character traits are best transferred to a young person's life by the example of someone with whom he or she has a heart connection. When a young person sees parents and church leaders exercising consistent faith, integrity, poise, disciplines, endurance, and courage—especially under the stresses of life—it's so much easier for him or her to know how to make these powerful traits his or her own. Grace-based homes and churches are deliberate about building these into the hearts of the next generation—both formally and informally.

For an in depth look into how to transfer these six character traits into a child's heart, you might want to look at the book *Raising Kids Who Turn Out Right*, (Kimmel, Family Matters) at *shop.familymatters.net*. Incidentally, there's a great hint for effective parenting and family ministry in the title of this book. We want to raise kids who *turn out* right. Most Christian parents and youth pastors get preoccupied with raising kids who *go through* childhood right. Grace assumes that children will struggle with wrong behavior, but doesn't overreact to it. It corrects it as it goes along, but its true focus is on building character into the child's heart—deliberately and patiently—that will serve them well when it's their turn to lead the next generation.

Dimension 4: Aiming children at true greatness.

The fourth dimension of a grace-based family deals with our children's future. The standard mistake Christian parents make is concentrating their efforts on raising children who grow up to be *successful*. The problem with this plan is that it's already dead-on-arrival spiritually because of how our culture quantifies success. The standard measurements for success are wealth, beauty, power, and fame.

That's why grades; SAT scores; the prestige of a college; the status of kid's friend's families; and where our children are in the athletic, academic, and social pecking order mean so much to some parents. They're assuming this is the fast track to a good income in the future. There is a lot of trauma exchanged in families over a child's looks, weight, and the appearance and pedigree of the people they want to marry. Being captain of . . . whatever and gaining public recognition for their efforts finishes out the picture. It's all about wealth, beauty, power, and fame. Although there's nothing wrong with any of these features of a successful life, per se, there are huge problems when they are encouraged by parents to be the sum total of a child's focus.

What Christian parents don't seem to realize is that God places no special value on wealth, beauty, power, and fame in the Bible. These four goals have no bearing on whether or not a child will grow up to be happy or have any eternal impact. On top of that, parents don't even need God's help in preparing their children for a future measured by these superficial standards of success. Unbelieving parents aim their kids at these same four goals all the time—and do a good job of seeing them achieved. These four goals place enormous stress on both the parent and the child. The saddest part of this effort is that these parents don't realize that when it comes to their child's future, they're aiming *low*.

It makes so much more sense to aim our children at true greatness. In Matthew 20:25-28 Jesus said, "You know that the rulers of the Gentiles lord it over them, and their high officials exercise authority over them. Not so with you. Instead, whoever wants to become great among you must be your servant, and whoever wants to be first must be your slave—just as the Son of Man did not come to be served, but to serve, and to give his life as a ransom for many."

Based on this passage and other things Jesus said about what's most important, I'd like to suggest a definition of true greatness as follows:

True Greatness—a passionate love for Jesus Christ that shows itself in an unquenchable love and concern for others.

Parents and family ministries who raise their children aimed at true greatness—focused upwards and outwards—automatically minimize so many of the tensions that plague families and churches wrapped up in the success delusion. Success focuses on self; true greatness focuses on God and sees the needs of others. Success breeds siblings rivalry and toxic comparison; true greatness encourages respect for siblings and a desire to pursue the other person's best interests. Success drives church departments to a silo mentality; true greatness unites them around the rallying call of grace-based relationships that want to see all departments thrive.

There are four wonderful qualities of true greatness that parents and family ministries can work in concert to transfer into the heart of children. Although there are specific things parents and church leaders can do to demonstrate these qualities as well as require of their kids when it comes to living out these qualities, the greatest victory is when these become the genuine outflow of their child's personal relationship with Jesus.

The qualities of true greatness are:

1. **A humble heart**—a reverence for God and respect for others.

   "Do nothing out of selfish ambition or vain conceit. Rather in humility value others above yourselves, not looking to your own interests but to the interests of others" (Philippians 2:3-4).

2. **A grateful heart**—an appreciation for what they have been given and Who has given it.

   "Give thanks in all circumstances; for this is God's will for you in Christ Jesus" (1 Thessalonians 5:18).

3. **A generous heart**—a great delight in sharing with others what God has entrusted to you.

"Give, and it will be given to you. A good measure, pressed down, shaken together and running over, will be poured into your lap. For with the measure you use, it will be measured to you" (Luke 6:38).

4. **A servant's heart**—a willingness and joy to take action in order to help someone else.

"Truly I tell you, whatever you did for one of the least of these brothers and sisters of mine, you did for me" (Matthew 25:40).

God's grace fast tracks hearts into alignment with His heart—more effectively and efficiently than anything else we have to offer. How could it not? When our kids are being influenced by parents and leaders at church who have a passionate love for Jesus that shows itself in an unquenchable love and concern for *others*, relationships rock! This is especially true when those parents and leaders braid those relationships together through the disarming and charming power of humble hearts, grateful hearts, generous hearts, and servants' hearts. A sidebar benefit to all of this is that we grease the skids for our children's future *success!*

These qualities do more to insure our children will grow up to meet their highest potential than any academic resume or athletic accomplishment ever can. These are exactly the kinds of qualities the marketplace is looking for when it comes to the higher levels of executive management. Success in the more prestigious levels of business is less about skill and more about the *kind* of person the leader is—someone who is trustworthy, positive, magnanimous, others-oriented, and caring.

Aiming a child at a future of true greatness also sets them up to have much more successful relationships in the future—especially when it comes to their marriage. That's because truly great hearts tend fall in love and marry other truly great-hearted people. And grace-based people are much lower maintenance when it comes to marriage. Raising kids for true greatness through the power of God's grace is one of the greatest wedding gifts you could ever give your children and one of the best ways to ensure that churches will be filled with truly great families.

For a deeper study of true greatness and tools for transferring the four qualities of true greatness into a child's heart, you might want to look more deeply at *Raising Kids for True Greatness* (Kimmel, Thomas Nelson Publishers) at *shop.familymatters.net.*

A COMPREHENSIVE AND COHESIVE BIG PICTURE

What God's grace does is provide a comprehensive and cohesive big picture for all of the other things we do as parents and church leaders. It also gives all of these other things credibility—biblical training, life coaching, theological savvy, relational etiquette, intellectual balance, and correction.

This house built by grace sets the limits on our pride, arrogance, and selfishness. When parents and churches share this same philosophical starting point, their strategies and tactics are more likely to be carried out in rhythm with God's gracious heart. Parents and churches that treat each other the way God treats them are more likely to minimize relational drama and be more equipped to recover from missteps faster.

There's one other thing that happens to parents and church leaders who allow God's grace to format the way they live out relationships with the people around them. It takes away fear. This is partly the result of the assumed requirement of grace-based living: living your life in complete trust on God. When we fear God properly, we hardly fear anyone or anything else at all. This diminished sense of fear is also the result of looking at people through the "grace lens." It tends to see past their quirky packaging, internal "issues," and bad behavior to the deeper needs of their heart.

The comprehensive and cohesive big picture of grace-based relationships is far more than a gift to the kids; it's a gift to marriages, friendships, staff, and volunteers that make up the church.

Incidentally, if someone handed me a napkin and said, "Draw a big picture plan for strong marriages," I'd sketch out the exact same house. How about a big picture philosophy, strategy, and tactics for a healthy church? I'd sketch out the exact same house. All we've been learning in this chapter is what God's grace looks like lived out in real time, up close and personal, with sweat all over it.

WHEN GRACE FRAMES THE BIGGER PICTURE

It's easy to slip into the trap of moving from the simple to the complex when we are trying to transfer faith into the next generation. Grace goes the other direction. It takes our challenges and distills them down to far more simple and manageable issues. In the long run, we can do more to bring hope and healing to the people we love and the families we serve by showing them the bigger picture of a life formatted by God's grace. By embracing God's grace as the driving feature of our relationships with each other we automatically create a comfort zone between everyone; an inclination towards each other's best interests. Nobility. Trust. Favor.

Maybe you feel you have a lot of catching up to do. Get in line. Most people do. But by embracing the grace of God in your life or your church's staff, you encourage the people you love to want to do the same. God's grace, living itself out in us and through us, automatically helps others get a better handle on their problems.

Grace is a wonderful prescription. That's because grace is a synonym for *favor*. It's also saturated with hope. When grace is formally embraced and collectively focused on through formal teaching and mutual encouragement, there is no stopping the impact God can have through everyone involved in the dance.

You've just been given a crash course in grace-based families. For a much more comprehensive look at these four dimensions the nice folks at Family Matters have created all that a church or parents need to turn grace from a pleasant concept into the DNA behind everything they do. Family Matters has a three-part DVD curriculum called *Grace Based Parenting, Parts I, II, and III* that provides the perfect way to make God's grace the atmosphere of everything you're doing. It's ideal and complete for small group and Sunday classroom interactive learning. You can learn all about it at *GraceBasedParenting.com*.

Nothing is simple. And years of damage aren't going to go away with a crash course on grace. But they'll never go away until God's grace is moved from a nice concept to the defining nature of family relationships and family ministries. Helping parents and church leaders understand the grace-based model of parenting gives them quantifiable as well as attractive goals for their relationship with their next generation. It gives them a reason to smile again.

ENDNOTES

[1] Neil Postman, *The Disappearance of Childhood*, (Delacorte Press: New York. 1982), p. xi.

[2] 2 Corinthians 12:9.

[3] 1 Peter 4:8.

[4] Carol Lea Mueller (Editor). *The Quotable John Wayne: The Grit and Wisdom of an American Icon*. (New York: The Taylor Publishing), p. 48.

CHAPTER 7

A GRACE FOR ALL SEASONS

O ften ideas make more sense when seen in a bigger context. With this in mind, some background may be in order.

God calls most pastors to minister to a particular church. He reserves a handful to minister to *the* Church in general. I'm part of that smaller group. Maybe it's because God doesn't trust me with a local church much longer than a weekend. I do my best to make sure it's not that. Actually, I think I understand the role this smaller group of pastors plays in the bigger story of *the* Church as well as a particular local church. Our job is to do the work that a typical pastor would love to do but can't because he or she is up to his or her elbows in the goo of people's broken lives.

Among other things, I feel my responsibility is to do homework for overworked servants of the Lord. I often picture them starting their week with every intention of pouring at least 15 hours of preparation into their Sunday sermon or their primary weekly lesson. But the sheep have a different agenda. For one thing, some sheep have teeth. A typical pastor has to factor some time into his or her standard week just to bandage up from nips and tears received from the unsatisfied. And then, between marrying, burying, coming alongside the sick, refereeing some conflicts, cheering on the faithful, and rescuing someone from the consequences of dumb choices, many pastors are fortunate if they get 15 minutes to focus their thoughts and frame their words for Sunday. Yet, they're still expected to pound a solid double or triple every time they walk up to the pulpit. That's why, in so many of the books I've written, I've tried to write chapters that are outlined, biblically annotated, and illustrated—a chapter that a pastor can easily grab on Saturday afternoon or evening and have something encouraging to say the next morning.

And God has not spared me the nips and tears, marrying, burying, refereeing, cheerleading, and rescuing responsibilities. Those are part of any person's life that is called into a ministry position—and I have the scars to prove it. Yet, although my typical week requires me to call audibles, just like most pastors, I've still had the ability to focus my studies in an area that, hopefully, allows me to go to depths and widths that most pastors would love to go to if they didn't have so many other demands on their docket. My job, then, is to come alongside the church and family with help that makes burdens lighter, congregations healthier, and, hopefully, lives better.

THUS GRACE

Too often local and domestic churches are either missing or seriously struggling to maintain the atmosphere of grace that was supposed to be permeating all of their teaching and relationships. When I started in ministry, I especially saw it missing in the rank-and-file families showing up for church each Sunday. And, sadly, I noticed that many church staffs struggled to make God's grace the prevailing feature of the relationships within their operations. I've been in churches with "Grace" in the name, but, man, oh, man, it was hard to find it when you slipped through the front door.

I don't say this as an indictment. Nor is it a putdown. I think it's just the *nature* of human nature. We're quick to embrace the part of the story that's easiest to quantify—like orthodoxy and biblical truth—but struggle to wrap our hearts around that part of the story that requires us to be more honest about our fragile and selfish natures and more forthright about how these foibles blur our faith picture. God's grace was supposed to be the part of the story that neutralized these tendencies. But grace doesn't allow itself to be embraced as an academic exercise. It requires humility, brokenness, and an almost reckless surrender to God's transforming impact in our lives.

So, for more than 35 years, I've studied God's Word with a special lens over my eyes as I read. I wanted to see how the *truth* of God and the *grace* of God are simultaneously present in what we teach, how we lead, and how we love each other within our church and personal family.

During this time, I've also been attached to the same local church. I've had the privilege of serving within that church the entire time. For a while I was on its staff as its youth pastor. But, when my calling moved me to be available to the church-at-large, I still remained connected to my local church in what I hoped were substantive ways, utilizing my spiritual gifts. I've taught classes to young families. I've served as an ad hoc staff member. And I've served several terms as an elder. During this time, our church moved from a weekly attendance of 600 to 6,000.

MOVEMENTS COME; MOVEMENTS GO

What I've been sharing in this book is not something that just appeared overnight but something that has been forged during three decades of study and ministry. I say none of this in order to receive an accolade. I don't think any accolades are deserved. I'm just doing what God assigned me to do—just like so many other people in His service. The reason I'm saying this is to put the grace-based message in a bigger context. This isn't a "movement" within family ministry.

I'm leery of movements—at least church ones.

Most people of faith assume a large-scale movement is invariably the work of the Holy Spirit. Actually, the movement of the Holy Spirit is more about cleaning up and clarifying the message than it is in making a radical shift in the way we do ministry or family. That's because, when our message is clear and complete, there's no need for movements. A clear and complete message yields balanced lives. Plus, God can use all kinds of circumstances and ministry styles to carry out His Kingdom agenda. When the Holy Spirit truly moves, He *reforms*. So, if anything, a clear, complete, balanced, and unencumbered message creates *reformation*, not movement. There's a huge difference.

God's transforming grace was never meant to be a "flash point" (i.e., *movement*) on Church history's calendar, but an anchor tenant of the gospel. All we're talking about in this book is the way it was supposed to be *from the beginning*.

Most man-made ecclesiastical movements are short-lived. That's because most "movements" are usually a *reaction* to something that has gone too far in a certain direction.

I'm not saying that God can't use movements. What I'm saying is that most movements, at least within the church, tend to be a man-made reaction to the way things are or aren't. If we had been truly listening to the Holy Spirit all along, the situation to which we are reacting probably wouldn't exist, at least not in our churches and personal lives.

I've been around long enough to see a lot of movements come and go through the church: The "Men's" movement, the "Culture War" movement, the "Political Action" movement, the "Church Growth" movement, the "Emergent Church" movement, to name a few. These movements were more "American" in nature than spiritual. And these movements, though started with good intentions, have left a great deal of human wreckage in their wake. Reactionary movements tend to do that. And although there are still remnants of these movements, the man-made residue from well-intended but often misguided passions has left a bad taste in a lot of people's mouths. The Holy Spirit's *reforming* work NEVER does that.

I remember when the "Hunker Down" movement came out of the woodwork. It wasn't called that, and probably wouldn't appreciate me using that terminology to describe it, but that's what it was about. It had its roots in the 1960s but picked up traction the beginning of the 1970s and was at Mach 2 with its hair on fire by the time this new century came around. The focus of this movement was on how corrupted and vile our culture was—and what a dangerous place it was to try to raise a family. The goal of this movement was to create alternative ways to live within this culture without having to necessarily *engage* it as a family. What came out of it was a kind of parallel universe in which Christian families could exist without having to expose their kids to the harsh frontlines of the contaminated world around them. Safe, country club-type churches with a crowded calendar of family-friendly programs and alternative ways of educating their kids became the mainstays of this movement.

It's now produced a generation of offspring who ask some extremely difficult questions about its starting presuppositions and man-shaped methodology. In the midst of this questioning was some honest soul-searching. What's refreshing is that on a *grand scale* key leaders within this movement have come to the recognition that it was:

† Letting fear have too prominent a role in framing its thinking.

† Letting heavy-handed leadership at home have too much unbridled control.

† Letting man-made suggestions too often morph into biblical non-negotiables.

† Letting self-righteousness dominate too much of its public brand.

The most substantive conclusion that has risen out of its soul-searching is that the *grace of God*—as a *fundamental* and *quantifiable* feature of *everything*—was the biggest missing ingredient from the beginning. It's obvious why it wasn't in place from the beginning. Fear and grace *don't* co-exist very well. Grace assumes trust and confidence in God's ability to protect us as well as help us thrive in the midst of the worst cultural contexts. Fear and trust are antinomies.

Yet, it is exciting to see how, out of some of the disappointing results of this movement, solid, well-balanced biblical steps are being taken to bring a gracious equilibrium into the middle of it. Key leaders are seeing they gave too much legitimacy to their personal fears as leaders of families and churches. They were trying to take families back to a photoshopped, idealistic time in America's history that, if you actually know America's history, NEVER EXISTED. It's been so heartening to watch the grassroots of this movement come back to the grace that saved them and want to learn how to let it now define the relationships it's trying to impact.

As evidenced in so many emails, blog comments, and personal conversations, one of the most heartening adjustments of this movement has been in homeschooling. It's been great to see this tool for families (which is most likely here to stay) recognize the glaring need for a gracious atmosphere within the bigger context of this educational option. Homeschool parents are embracing the fear-less, grace-based way of raising and educating kids in wholesale numbers. They're simply coming back to a feature that was always meant to be part of our center-stage presentation of our faith.

MODELS COME; MODELS GO

Grace-based parenting isn't a "model" of ministry either. There are places for "models." In fact, I think models of ministry are foregone conclusions. If you have any kind of structure and predictability to the madness you call ministry in your church or home, then it can probably be given a "model" name. There's nothing wrong with this. Models help us get on the same page and move more effectively and efficiently in the same direction.

But a model is only as reliable as the person or church using it. Just about any model can be embraced, while still allowing all kinds of flawed philosophy to dominate it. That's because models don't define message; they define method (strategy and tactics).

For instance, one of my favorite models is known as Faith@ Home. It has many variations and nuances, but the bottom line is in its name. Nothing makes more sense to me than getting parents to step up and carry the heavy spiritual water at home with their kids. But, once again, what if the parents are dictators on steroids? What if they're heavy-handed and egotistic? What if they're controlled by their fears or defined by their inadequacies? What if their understanding of the role of a man or woman is an aberration of what Scripture actually teaches? What if they believe the local church should play no role in the family?

The answer is obvious. It doesn't matter how wonderful a particular model is; under these conditions, it's not going to work very well. That's because regardless of the "movement" we follow or the family ministry "model" we embrace, if we don't have a philosophical commitment to have it guided by God's truth and tempered by His grace, then we're going to spend billions of dollars, lose years of sleep, and cry lakes of tears for little reward.

A GRACE SHOUT-OUT

There are lots and lots more voices within Christianity that have come to this same conclusion regarding the missing role of grace in our greater evangelical message. These voices are coming from all of the major denominations and disciplines of biblical understanding. Both reformed and dispensational thinkers are voicing a more center-stage role of God's grace when it comes to defining the nature of relationships. Some of the leading church planters and mega-church leaders in the world are articulating a biblical priority of God's grace.

Christian schools are picking up the chorus too. Once again, something that started as a reactionary "movement" has now had a generation to use as a benchmark for its impact. They've had to do some soul searching too. More and more, leadership and teachers are seeing that God's grace has too often only received lip service. They now want to make His gracious heart a substantive extension of everything that happens within their system.[1]

Probably the biggest voice for a commitment to grace-based relationships is coming from the regular people sitting in the seats at church on Sunday. When they hear the message of grace-based relationships, they relax, they feel like they have come home and realize this is what was missing all along. This is especially so when it comes to how they live out their relationships with the people closest to them—their spouse, children, and grandchildren. There is an anthem of grace becoming a glorious chorus throughout Christendom.

Perhaps what's going on here is the Holy Spirit tugging on hearts across the board to reform homes and churches that became too focused on their man-made dilemmas, too defined by their man-made thinking, and too enmeshed in their man-made systems.

GRIDIRON LOGIC

Darcy and I were having lunch with a longtime acquaintance. He also happened to have played for the Colts while they were still in Baltimore. His name is Joe Erhmann. During his stint of cracking heads in the NFL, God got hold of his heart. After hanging up his shoulder pads for good, Joe spent several years looking deeper into the Scripture in seminary. Since then, Joe has had quite a track record of living out his faith on the front lines of the cause. God has given Joe a special passion to step into the gap on behalf of those getting short-sheeted in life.

Joe has a way of cutting through a lot of the back noise within the Christian world. Sometimes our fears and prejudices incline us into a mode of thinking that unwittingly denies us a greater grasp of the relationship we're supposed to be enjoying with Christ.

Joe told us at that lunch, "I notice three categories of churches. There are 'Word' churches. Their primary focus is on the powerful preaching and teaching of the Scripture. It's very important to these churches that a believer have a sophisticated understanding of biblical truth, doctrine, orthodoxy, and theology to guide their lives." Bible churches are very strong in this category.

"The second kind of church I've observed is what I'd call 'Wonder' churches. This is a church that seems keenly aware of the greater battle going on between the forces of evil and Almighty God. They also see Satan and his minions playing a more intimate role in the negative features of everyday life—like sickness, injury, and lifestyle setbacks. It's not uncommon for you to experience passionate prayer for the moving of the Holy Spirit and evidence of His presence in their worship experience." Charismatic and Pentecostal churches come to mind when I think of these kinds of churches.

"Then there's the third kind of church I like to refer to as the 'Work' church. This is a church that is extremely sensitive to the distress going on within the human drama around them. They see poverty, high control, abuse, and injustice and are quick to jump into the middle of it and do something about it. In the process of rolling up their sleeves and trying to bring health and comfort to the people trapped in this distress, they're not afraid to take a public stand as a church and call the powers that be into account if they're at all responsible for creating or encouraging this distress." The Catholic Church has traditionally played this role throughout church history.

Then Joe leaned back in his chair, looked at Darcy and me and said, "Word churches, Wonder churches, and Work churches. Question: Which of those three is the church *supposed* to be?"

The answer just about knocked me out of my chair. It's supposed to be ALL of them! And it's supposed to be all of them *simultaneously*—in *balance* and *harmony.*

But because some Wonder churches might slip over the line and supplant God's power and presence with a man-made, signs-and-wonders peep show, Word churches, not wanting to be guilty by association, overreact to this aberration and end up with a suspicious attitude towards most supernatural work.

Or a Work church, in the process of trying to impact social or political systems that oppress people, either teams with others who have no regard for Christ, or hold back on articulating the source of the love that even inclines them towards kindness. Next thing you know, the Wonder and Word churches distance themselves from that kind of overt involvement in addressing injustice lest they become guilty by association of a watered-down social gospel.

Or a Word church loses its way in an otherwise passionate appreciation for the Scripture and ends up worshiping the Bible rather than the God of the Bible, drawing blood with fellow believers over the "wording" of the Bible at the expense of "oneness" that their relationship with the true Word of God—Jesus—is supposed to promote. They become Bible *institutes* rather than Bible *churches*. Next thing you know, the Work church or Wonder church is going light on the serious study of the Scripture lest they get mistaken for those biblical pinheads down the street who yell at them a lot.

Obviously, I've exaggerated this a bit to make a point. But if you've at all been around the ecclesiastical block you know that I'm not stereotyping what is normally the exception but rather too often the rule.

GRACE TO THE RESCUE

Among the many things that make grace so amazing, it's the way it brings balance and harmony to churches and families that want to represent the whole counsel of God.

From cover-to-cover, the story of God's involvement with the human race consistently involves the braided trilogy of God's Word, His Wonder, and His Work. Jesus was the living, breathing reality of these three priorities. His incarnation *is* God's Word, God's Wonder, and God's Work wrapped in swaddling clothes. The cross was their magna carta; the empty tomb was their crowning glory. The quills of John, Peter, and Paul validated them. To operate as a church or a family with any one priority at the expense of the other is to miss God's greater good for ourselves as well as the role He desires to play through us.

That's why making God's heart of grace the philosophical starting point of our relational priorities within our churches and families is so crucial. When God's grace is purposefully and actively lived out through us, all three of these biblical priorities rise to prominence within our hearts. God's grace demands a commitment to the orthodox authority of God's Word. God's grace can't be experienced, let alone maintained, without the obvious wonder of His power and presence showing up in our daily lives.

And the litmus test that God's transforming grace is truly a part of our life is the "others-orientation" work and outward focus we naturally have—especially for people who are out-gunned. Grace can't sit still or stay quiet in the presence of people in great need.

When God's grace is given its proper priority in our churches and homes, we obey the Word of God, we enjoy the Wonder of God, and we enthusiastically do the Work of God—all the time!

FROM CONTEXT TO CONCRETE

This contextual discussion on the priority of God's grace has been greasing the skids for something extremely cool—at least I hope you'll see it that way. Grace makes it easy to frame a comprehensive strategy for the work of a church's family ministry as well as the role of parents grooming the next generation of Jesus followers.

That's what this whole book has been leading up to. I'll be glad to show you what I mean . . . in the next chapter.

ENDNOTES

[1] That's another way the nice folks at Family Matters have stepped up to the need. They offer a great "in service" way to get everyone in the Christian school (administration and teachers) to turn God's grace into the culture in which they operate. For more information, contact Family Matters at *familymatters.net.*

CHAPTER 8

A FAMILY MINISTRIES MANDATE

I t was a dark and stormy night . . . . well, actually, it was a hot and dry Thursday evening. But at least it was dark. The elder board at our church was meeting. Among their discussions was an urgent need to hire a staff person who could meet the demands for more deliberate biblical and spiritual coaching of our families. The consensus was that we had come to the point where we'd be a much better ally and asset to the divergent types of families showing up Sunday after Sunday if we had a highly qualified leader to cheer them on—full-time.

Although genuine family ministry is the role of all pastors of a church, as well as the parents showing up, when you have *thousands* of families turning out each week, and many of them on life-support spiritually, it's a bit naïve to think a church can cover all of the bases thoroughly without some specialization.[1]

That's when a request was passed down from the senior pastor, as well as the chairman of the elder board, that they'd like to form a search committee for this new member of the pastoral team. Motion, seconded, all in favor say "Ah!"—and they'd like me to head up that search committee.

Individual elders serve at the behest of the elder board and the leadership of the church. So I said okay.

But I knew this was going to be easier to decree at a board meeting than to make happen in reality.

I gathered some people around me to form this search committee. My focus was people, who not only had a passionate love for Christ and an unquenchable love and concern for others, but who also had a tender place in their heart for healthy and strong families. One more thing, I wanted people on the search committee who "got" grace.

Among this group was one of my life-long friends, Dr. John Trent. John and I met back in graduate school and have served as iron-sharpening-iron type friends in our personal lives and ministry lives ever since. John is one of the best tactically gifted voices in the country when it comes to family ministry.

GROUNDWORK

One of the biggest mistakes churches make when looking to fill a position on their staff is to immediately start searching for a person with the gifting and availability to assume a position rather than doing the gritty hard work of defining that particular ministry. I'm not talking about defining "what" they do. That's obvious. I'm talking about that bigger philosophical, strategic story that gives everyone involved a clearer understanding of *why we're heading a certain direction and what course we want to take to get there.* This gives the person hired a clear track. When churches fail to do this, they're confined by whatever that servant brings to the table. What he or she brings may be great, but it might not necessarily be what the church really needs or wants. Nice people get unnecessarily hurt. A lot of heartache, disappointment, unmet expectations, and failure could be avoided if the church just did the forward-thinking type of work that hiring a pastor genuinely requires.

I told the elder board we had some groundwork to do. Once it was done, we'd begin our search. Before we could define what we were looking for in a family *minister,* we'd have to define exactly what we meant by family *ministry.*

I mentioned that the couples who made up this search committee were people who "get" grace. Many of them were couples I had known and taught for more than a decade. They had a share in the architectural drawings of what came to be known as the grace-based plan for parenting. Over those years, while teaching them, many of the books that unpack this strategy were written.

These couples gave more than lip service to a commitment to living out God's grace within their families. They were card-carrying ambassadors for the cause of homes guided by God's truth, while simultaneously tempered by His grace. And they had a collection of children, who are living illustrations of the validity and effectiveness of grace-based parenting.

Laying out the big picture of what we meant by family ministry was fairly easy for them. With a goes-without-saying commitment to biblical orthodoxy at the foundational level, they wanted to make sure the end goal was designed to create and maintain an atmosphere of grace that was introduced to you in Chapter 4. They knew you can teach biblical orthodoxy all you want, but if there isn't an atmosphere that represents the tender heart of God, it's not going to pay the kind of long-term spiritual dividends we'd prefer—and that Jesus' work for us on the cross deserves.

They also wanted to make sure the people who followed us as leaders of our church in the future understood why we designed things the way we did. We wanted to leave them easy tracks to follow . . . . if they so chose.

HOMES THAT DON'T FAKE, CHURCHES THAT DON'T POSE

Let me step away from the search committee story for a second to make an overarching observation. There are at least three responsibilities that spiritually balanced homes and churches carry out consistently and simultaneously. They *share*, they *care*, and they *grow*. Let me use a metaphor of a hospital to try to get our heads around this. When churches and Christian homes are walking in step with the gospel, there are three types of hospital services going on.

Delivery Room/Nursery (sharing): Families and churches, committed to God's grace story, often hear the passionate and exciting wails of people who have just come to life in Christ or the baby-talk of new believers in the background. Evangelism is supposed to be a standard feature of healthy, grace-based churches and families. In other words, both the *domestic* and the *local* church are supposed to be active sources of God's redeeming message. When the analogy is regarding an actual family, we're not limiting evangelism to the kids being raised inside that home (although that is of highest importance), but seeing the much larger role of a family as being a redemptive influence on the people that surround it and interact with it. This doesn't require a family to overtly jam Jesus down the throat of everyone that crosses its path (once again, I'm exaggerating to make a point!). But because they live out the love of God to each other and through each other, even under the stresses of life, God is going to naturally use them to touch other people's lives. And even when they get life wrong, the way they recover through the power of God's grace also gives credence to the transforming power of the gospel. When it's a local church we're talking about, it's like the same thing—only on spiritual steroids.

Emergency Room (caring): Grace-based churches and homes should be one of the safest and most dependable places that people can turn to in order to work through all of the drama and junk of their lives. Sometimes we're the patients. Most of the time we're the orderlies, nurses, technicians, and doctors. The spiritual growth and biblical knowledge we accrue along the way is supposed to give us an enthusiastic *desire* to be available to be used whenever and wherever God needs us. That's what grace-based homes and churches do.

Fitness Center (growing): Maintaining spiritual fitness is just like its physical counterpart. It's determined by what you eat and don't eat and by an exercise regimen you actually follow. Healthy homes and churches work in sync to make sure everyone who is willing has a way to strengthen their spiritual muscles and then use those muscles to serve others for God's glory.

Yet, deliberate evangelism is a struggle for most churches—especially when it comes to establishing it as the default mode for the typical church member. It's non-existent as standard operating procedure for most Christian families outside their own children.

Most people in the spiritual emergency rooms prefer to be the patient. Too often Christians are tempted to lie around on gurneys and have someone coddle them, even if they only have the equivalent of a spiritual paper cut.

And when it comes to life in the fitness center, this is where the biggest problem happens. There's a reason that Paul both warned and challenged us regarding the improper versus proper attitude toward the truth of God when he said that, "knowledge puffs up while love builds up."[2] Too many people want to brag about their great personal trainers and state-of-the-art fitness equipment, but most of the time just stand around looking in the mirrors admiring their beautifully shaped spiritual booties. They take pride at how many verses they've memorized and how many theological questions they can answer but look at you like you're evil incorporated when you ask them to roll up their sleeves and do bedpan duty in the spiritual ER. They give you the "who me?" look when you suggest they actually *share* some of the verses they've memorized the next time some distraught person at work confides in them regarding their problems.

"What! I don't know enough to do that. That's for the professionals! That's what they're paid for. Listen, I just love God's Word. I want to spend the rest of my life just basking in it." The whole concept of being doers of the Word and not just hearers of it, deluding yourself[3] doesn't record with them.

Let me give you an example of what I'm talking about. One New Year's Eve, Darcy and I were invited to join three other couples for dinner at an elegant restaurant. There was a great band playing in the background and everyone was in a celebration mood. Someone in our group thought it might be a cool idea to go around our table and share what he or she most enjoyed about their past year—from a spiritual perspective. (For the record, it wasn't me who made that suggestion!)

The guy next to me went first. What he was most excited about was (I'm not making this up) the *four* Bible studies he attended each week and then the capstone of it all was sitting on Sunday morning and being fed by our pastor.

I knew these Bible studies. They're strong gatherings that meet throughout our city either before work or at lunchtime. They're designed for businessmen and women, especially the non-churched ones, who are looking for answers to the messy situations in their life.

The guy next to me wasn't one of those God-seeking, messed-up businessmen. He had been going to church for 40 years. He was a very nice guy, but like many "nice" (read: "safe") believers, a bit reluctant to step into the middle of the fray and switch on his spiritual lights. The Bible studies he was attending were "celebrity" Bible studies, meaning, they were taught by highly gifted or famous Bible teachers in our town. If anyone could brag about his personal spiritual trainers, this guy could.

No one had mentioned to me that we weren't supposed to comment on someone's spiritual cupcake from the past year. I turned to the guy and said, "You know what I'd wish for you next year, if I ruled the world? That you'd keep attending church every Sunday and then pick one of those mid-week Bible studies to attend, drop the other three and start TEACHING one yourself." It was like I'd suddenly spit in everyone's drink.

Darcy suddenly got the urge to dance.

She insisted on me joining her on the dance floor where she discreetly pumped her fist and said, "Right on!"

MEDIOCRITY NEED NOT APPLY

These concerns played heavily into the priorities our search committee wanted to use to define our family ministry (and minister). We wanted to make sure we didn't create a family ministry that made it easy for people to stand spiritually still. And we didn't want to merely have a bunch of programs that encouraged parents to sub-contract their job to our church, either. Most of all, we didn't want to hire a glorified program director. We wanted to have a ministry that made it exciting to be a church and a family where the spiritual Delivery Rooms/Nurseries often had activity, the spiritual Emergency Rooms always had plenty of willing help, and the spiritual Fitness Center wasn't a place to see and be seen, but a place that prepped everyone for active duty on the front lines of the cause of Christ.

Our church has three words it uses to encourage every church participant to be doing these on a weekly basis:

- † Worship
- † Connect
- † Serve[4]

Not that I'm trying to be a namedropper or anything but, *Jesus* said, "'Love the Lord your God with all your heart and with all your soul and with all your mind.' This is the first and greatest commandment. And the second is like it: 'Love your neighbor as yourself'" (Matthew 22:37-39).

We show our love to and for God through *worship*. We worship Him by both giving to Him and receiving from Him. There are two types of neighbors we are called to love: our spiritual neighbors within the family of God,[5] and anyone else whose need we see and whose need we can meet.[6] Our church encourages everyone to *connect* weekly with fellow Christians to learn together and meet each other's needs, and to *serve* weekly each other as well as the greater needs of the community of our fellow man (whether next door, across town, or on the other side of the globe).

Worship, connecting, and serving were WHAT we were encouraging everyone in our church to do. Now, let me introduce four new words to you:

1. Value
2. Free
3. Empower
4. Aim

Those may not ring a bell with you yet, but they might if you remember back to our four dimensions of the grace-based strategy we unpacked in Chapter 5. These are four action words to capture the essence of those grace dimensions in our attitudes and actions toward our own family and our church family.

We **value** the people in our family and our church by using our words and actions to consistently meet their needs for:

✝ A secure love
✝ A significant purpose
✝ A strong hope

We **free** the people in our family and our church to be all God created them to be by gifting them with the:

- † Freedom to be different
- † Freedom to be vulnerable
- † Freedom to be candid
- † Freedom to make mistakes

We **empower** the people in our family and our church for life's greatest challenges by building into them the character traits of:

- † Faith
- † Integrity
- † Poise
- † Disciplines
- † Endurance
- † Courage

We **aim** the people in our family and our church at a life of passionately loving God and enthusiastically serving others by encouraging them to have a:

- † Humble heart
- † Grateful heart
- † Generous heart
- † Servant's heart

If *worship, connect,* and *serve* were WHAT we are encouraging our church members and families to do, then *value, free, empower,* and *aim* is HOW we were encouraging them to carry out WHAT they were doing. Without the four dimensions of a grace-based atmosphere describing the HOW, our strategy of *worship, connect,* and *serve* might accommodate any church and family configuration—even legalistic, nightmarish ones. That's why it was so important to our committee that we hang our strategy and tactics on the grace-based philosophy of relationships by articulating *exactly* how we wanted our family ministry to *feel* and *behave.*

TRAINING AND TOUCH POINTS

The rest of the plan fell together fairly easily. We wanted our family ministry to offer on-going, looping training when it comes to how grace-based parents lead their kids and how grace-based families treat each other.

And then we wanted to have specific ways the professional and lay-trained leadership within our church could come alongside parents to coach and encourage them in particular touch points of a child's journey through their youth. The leadership would do this for parents and kids two ways:

Intrinsically: By *valuing* them, *freeing* them, *empowering* them, and *aiming* them through the power of God's grace. We wanted to have a "culture of grace" permeating our professional and lay leadership in our church. Obviously, it's hard to make this happen if you don't have buy-in from the senior pastor and elder (or deacon) board. Fortunately, God's grace drives our senior pastor as he clearly leads us from the authority of God's truth. It's also the atmosphere that surrounds our elder board. So, the committee wanted to make sure that as leaders touched families in our church, they did so with a gracious kindness—whether they were teaching, counseling, or just loving on them. We knew a culture of grace within our church was the surest way to see Jesus taken home into our church's families.

Intentionally: Like most churches, ours has different ways to help a person (regardless of age) to worship, connect, and serve. Those would continue, albeit within a clearly defined culture of grace. Also, there were specific events and needs that families have in general and parents have in particular that we wanted to equip them to face within a grace-based atmosphere. They were:

- † Baby dedication (for some churches, it may be infant baptism).
- † Giving children a clear sense of blessing.
- † Educating and preparing children in the area of love, sex, and honor (ages 5-6 and up).
- † Dialing in on a child's unique personality bent (age 5 and up).
- † Training children in financial stewardship.
- † Marking a rite of passage (age 13).
- † Identifying spiritual giftedness.
- † Equipping them to be deliberate lights in their world (evangelism).
- † Providing a ceremony or some way to mark their preparation for launch into adulthood (age 16).
- † Putting their future marriage into perspective.
- † Preparing them to flourish spiritually in college.[7]

HEAVIER CROSSES

We also felt some families came to church with heavier weight on their shoulders. And there were others who couldn't come to church to get encouragement, even if they wanted to. We wanted to be able to come alongside them with more support. These would include single parents, adoptive parents, foster parents, parents of children with special needs, and missionary families.

But how could we put this together in such a way that would be easy for a parent to grasp and easy for a potential family pastor to wrap his or her arms around? Believe it or not, Mickey Mouse came to our rescue. In the next chapter, I'll show you how we put this all together in one document.

Here's the great thing: whether you have a church that is a typical family-based church but segmented by age groups; or a family-equipping style church that is organized by age but configured to call parents to be more active partners in discipling their kids; or you're a family-integrated church where you have intergenerational worship, Bible study, and discipleship, you can find much to apply in this seamless, overarching, grace-based plan.

Now here's the cool thing: Every part of this plan can be led by laypeople. So, if a paid family pastor isn't part of your church's priorities or budget, there's still a clear philosophy, strategy, and tactical plan you can embrace.

And here's the coolest thing: even if your church doesn't have the means or desire to come alongside you as a parent raising your family, this philosophy, strategy, and tactics can be carried out by any parent who wants to deliberately raise his or her kids the way God raises His kids—with grace!

ENDNOTES

[1] The handful of larger churches that do pull it off without a family pastor usually do so because their senior pastor is so focused on family as a priority and weighs in on it regularly as he addresses the congregation. Technically, they *are* a church with a full-time family pastor. He just happens to also be the senior pastor.

[2] 1 Corinthians 8:1.

[3] James 1:22.

[4] Churches have a lot of different ways to say the same thing (like: come, grow, go, etc.). Our church is not unique.

[5] John 15:12-14.

[6] Luke 10:27-37.

[7] Brian Haynes, in his excellent book *Shift*, has similar "legacy milestones" that he identifies in his family ministry model.

CHAPTER 9

THE ~~HAPPIEST~~ *MOST GRACIOUS* PLACE ON EARTH

It would be tempting to think that having a family ministry in a church is as simple as hiring a family pastor. But reality says otherwise. There are lots of churches that have family pastors but no true family ministry. Fortunately, the church I attend and the family ministry search committee I found myself on knew better than to assume something so important could be gained so easily. We knew that before we looked for a person to lead our family ministry, we needed to do the heavy lifting required to first *define* family ministry philosophically, strategically, and tactically. As a result of that work our search committee had a fairly good idea what we wanted our grace-based family ministry to look like and how we wanted it to express itself within our "worship, connect, serve" church vision. We spent several sessions hammering that all out. But how could we create a visual that would bring all of the parts together in one big seamless picture?

That's when someone mentioned his recent visit to Disneyland. Disneyland's (and Disneyworld's) tagline is: *The Happiest Place on Earth.* Obviously, if you've ever taken your kids there and actually spent 14 hours doing the equivalent of the "Iditirod of parenting" you might be inclined to take a can of spray paint and edit that tagline on their sign as you exit. A long day at Disneyland is demanding, yet families still line up at its gates every morning to subject themselves to that kind of physical and emotional pressure. Why? It's because Disneyland does what it does extremely well.

One of the ways it's organized itself is by dividing the park into different "lands": Tomorrowland, Adventureland, Fantasyland, and Frontierland, to name a few. When you slip from Tomorrowland into Adventureland, you don't wonder to yourself, *"Did I just leave Disneyland?"* You *know* you're still in Disneyland and always have been since you cleared the front gate. That's because there's a Disney *way* and Disney *feel* to everything you encounter inside *The Happiest Place on Earth.* However, each land has its own distinctives. The color palate, landscaping, names and types of rides, styles of the uniforms, names of the restaurants, and even the names of items on the menus align with the overarching theme of that particular "land."

Likewise, a typical church is made up of different "lands." There's worship, family, men's, women's, missions, outreach, etc. The way we saw it, our committee had been assigned the job of defining and designing "FamilyLand" at our church.

THE DISNEY FEEL AND WAY OF A CHURCH

I mentioned that there's a reason why people keep coming back to Disneyland year-after-year, decade-after-decade, from kids to grandkids. It's not the rides, and it's not the food. There are lots of theme parks with bigger roller coasters, scarier rides, and even tastier food. And many of them are easier on a family's budget than Disneyland. So why is it that Disneyland continues to be the first among equals? It's because of the Disney *way* of doing things and the Disney *feel* you experience when you're there. To hook the hoses up a bit more obviously to the vocabulary we've been using for our discussion on grace, we'd call it "the atmosphere of Disney" or the "Disney culture" you sense when you're there. From its look, the way the "cast members" treat you, the level of quality you find in even the minutest detail, it's all part of a grand experience.

As our committee discussed this phenomenon, we asked ourselves this question: What do we want people to "feel" when they come on our church campus or grow up in one of our church families? What is the "way" we want people to go about what they do when it comes to our professional and volunteer staff and the parents of our church? The answer to both questions was the same.

GRACE!

We want people to feel God's grace when they're at our church, we want them to sense God's grace when they engage any kind of professional or volunteer leader, and we want our children to experience God's grace coming from their parent(s).

This is where I have to give a shout out to Mickey Mouse. When you purchase your tickets at Disneyland, if you're not familiar with

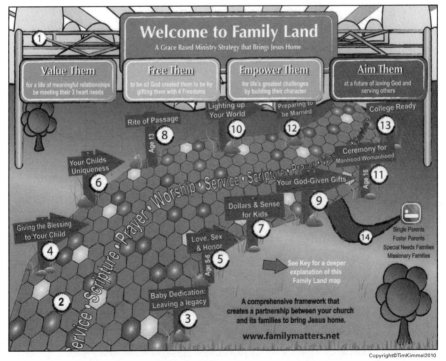

For a larger view, go to page 138 or *FamilyLand.FamilyMatters.net*.

what's inside, they hand you a cleverly designed map of the park. The various lands with their attractions, stores, and restaurants are all laid out for you in one, simple pamphlet.

We figured we could layout our design for our family ministry in a similar way. We called it, "Welcome to FamilyLand." (See prototype of what we did on page 109.)

It's gone through many changes and will continue to be developed. But if you want to see a more current version of the FamilyLand map go, right now, to *FamilyLand.FamilyMatters.net* and I'll give you a tour. Please don't go nuts studying the whole thing before I get to explain it. Do your best to restrain yourself and slip back here to let me lay out the big picture and its parts as we go along.

Incidentally, whether your church is family-based, family-equipping, family-integrated, or doesn't have a family priority at all (yet), this map can give you a great idea how to see a big picture philosophy, strategy, and tactics that engage your families with ministry that is driven by God's gracious heart.

A Few Important Notes Before We
Take a Quick Walk Through the FamilyLand Map

1. This FamilyLand Map is just one church's attempt to capture the essence of what they were trying to do with their family ministry. It isn't the first, only, or final word on anything. It's just a suggestion designed to hopefully get your own creative juices flowing.

2. This map is a liquid document. Our church, as well as Family Matters, is always trying to improve it. I suggest you revisit it often to learn of new tools available for its various features as well as upgrades to its overall concept.

3.   The FamilyLand Map can be used as a guide for both a church's family ministry as well as an individual parent who wants to conscientiously raise committed followers of Jesus. Some parents are equipped to walk their children through these different stages of spiritual development without any help from their church. But if, like most parents, they feel somewhat inadequate, it's nice to know their local church is willing to come alongside them with specific coaching and training in these vital points of development.

4.   The different points of interest on the map can be overseen by laypeople. In fact, these can be wonderful opportunities for folks to step up and serve their fellow family members at church. If you have a large enough paid staff, you might choose for certain staff members to "own" or be responsible for making sure the stations on the map are covered. But you can still staff the particular priority with laypeople.

5.   There are a lot of great tools already available through books and DVD studies that address many of the features on the map. That means, for many of them, it's not necessary to develop original curriculum. Because of that, both below and on the website, I'm going to list some of the pre-packaged tools I'm most familiar with; the ones I feel do the most thorough job as well as do it within a context of the power of God's grace.

Regarding this, you'll notice there are several references to tools created by Family Matters (with which I am connected). Family Matters has taken on the responsibility of creating tools for delivering God's message to the heart of church leaders, parents, and children within the atmosphere of His grace. Since God's grace plays such a huge role in the effectiveness of the relationships within churches and families, you'll see several options from this ministry.

There are other great tools for the ongoing training of children and young people in things like Bible knowledge, Scripture memory, apologetics, and biblical worldview. We're *assuming* these are standard tools and curriculums already utilized in most conscientious churches (and families). We're not listing those kinds of curriculums here because they address the continuing "training in truth" that churches/parents typically use with their children and young people. What we list on our FamilyLand map are the subjects germane to equipping parents to connect to the hearts of their children and best prepare those children (through a grace-based relationship) to grow up to be passionate followers of Jesus.

6. This map is meant to be an idea from which you can launch a tailor-made version of it for yourself or your church. The sign posts of FamilyLand represent the priorities our church felt were important for parents and children to focus on together. If the FamilyLand Map works as it stands, great! Help yourself. It's downloadable and free for the taking. Or maybe it just gets your creative juices flowing and you can take it to greater and better heights. However, if you choose to eliminate the atmosphere of grace from your overall family ministry plan (outlined on the signs at the top of the map), please do me a favor and don't mention to anyone that I, or my church, had anything to do with your final results.

7. A parent can merge on to FamilyLand at any time and become engaged at the touch point that is most applicable to his or her family situation. In fact, one of the most

attractive reasons to have a FamilyLand strategy is that parents in all stages of spirituality are looking for help raising their kids. If they discover a place where they can get wise and meaningful coaching when it comes to raising their kids, they're inclined to be teachable—even if they haven't darkened the doors of a church in ages. In this regard, having an overall plan like this for your church or family is a great evangelistic opportunity.

Incidentally, if a church wanted to, they could use the basic framework of this map (i.e., the four atmosphere of grace signs along the top and the cobblestone path) to create a similar map for their other ministries like Men's, Women's, Missions, Outreach, etc.

A WALK THROUGH FAMILYLAND

Let's work through the map by following the numbers. You'll notice, if you're online, that what follows is also featured in the expanded Key to the online FamilyLand map.

OVERVIEW: There are four general features of the FamilyLand Map:

✝ The signs at the top that define everything happening underneath them.

✝ A cobblestone path that represents a typical 18 year journey of a child through their youth.

✝ Sign posts marking strategic opportunities for parents to do some significant connecting to and equipping of their children for an adult life of faith.

✝ A "Rest Stop" that addresses the needs of families dealing with unique circumstances.

There are numbers that key in on specific parts of the map. Let's walk through them together.

**The Road Signs at the Top.** Of everything on this map, THESE FOUR SIGNS ARE THE MOST IMPORTANT. Take them off, tweak them in anyway that inclines them toward checklists, performance measurements, or theological downloads and you can kiss God's grace goodbye! These four signs of Value, Free, Empower, and Aim keep God's heart of grace exactly where it belongs—center stage in relationships just like it is in His relationship with us. Change them to "Scripture memory," "dressing to please God," "quiet times," "avoiding the wrong crowd," or anything like that and you're back to the business-as-usual methods of performance and sin management. God's heart of grace MUST define everything going on beneath those signs. God's grace is *why* we're even talking about raising Jesus followers.

Our family ministry search committee wanted to codify this anchor tenant of our plan so that whomever we brought in to lead us would have no doubt where we were coming from. We wanted the POWER and PRESENCE of God's gracious love permeating everything we did and every bit of truth about God we would attempt to implant in our children's hearts.

These signs correspond to the four-part theology of grace you were introduced to in the house illustration in Chapter 6. They represent how God's saving grace should redefine us as followers of Jesus. They articulate what Christ is doing for His children.

REMEMBER: *Grace-Based Parenting is simply treating your children the way God treats His!*

For more understanding of this house illustration as it relates to a grace-based strategy for families go to *parenting.familymatters.net.*

Like overarching directional signs, they define the culture, context, and course of everything happening below them. These signs not only signify the way parents should be treating their children, but also the way the church professional and volunteer staff should treat each other. When a parent or child interacts with church leadership, they should feel like they are being valued, freed up, empowered, and aimed toward greatness.

Value Them by meeting their three inner needs for:

✝ A secure love

✝ A significant purpose

✝ A strong hope

Free Them by creating an atmosphere within the home where everyone is given:

✝ The freedom to be different

✝ The freedom to be vulnerable

✝ The freedom to be candid

✝ The freedom to make mistakes

Empower Them by building character into their hearts, specifically the character traits of:

✝ Faith

✝ Integrity

✝ Poise

✝ Disciplines

✝ Endurance

✝ Courage

Aim Them at a future of true greatness. True Greatness is defined as a "passionate love for Jesus that shows itself in an unquenchable love and concern for others." The qualities of a truly great follower of Jesus are:

† Humility

† Gratefulness

† Generosity

† A servant's spirit

② **The Cobblestone Path.** This path is the thoroughfare that parents and children follow through the "youth years." Four words make up the center striping of this cobblestoned path: worship, service, Scripture, and prayer. We're assuming that all of the normal teaching on Bible, doctrine, orthodoxy, apologetics, and worldview are still in place in the children and youth training being offered by the church and within conscientious families of faith. Typical Christian churches and Christian homes expose and involve children in these four pillars of our faith walk.

Additionally, you'll notice that some of the colors of the cobblestone correspond to the colors of the four signs at the top. This represents the fact that God's grace needs to be the defining element along the path of family ministry. It needs to be permeating all of the worship, service, Scripture, and prayer that are going on in our church and church's families. These colored cobblestones also represent the ongoing priority of training in grace offered by the church.

There are two great ways to keep this grace strategy front and centered in the parent and children's lives.

First: The pastoral staff of the church need to be committed to operating with each other, as well as the people of the congregation, according to these four tenants of applied relational grace: meeting each others inner needs, setting each other's hearts free, demonstrating well-defined character, and living a life focused on true greatness. Pettiness, territorialism, exclusivity, protectionism, gossip, scarcity thinking, arrogance, and comparison must once and for all leave the church offices.

Second: Parents need to be taught the grace-based strategy through ongoing training in marriage and parenting. This doesn't mean an occasional conference or sermon series every couple of years but rather deliberate and repeated small group and Sunday school enrichment hour studies, specifically designed to help people embrace God's grace at home. Every adult is *encouraged* to attend the studies provided either through small groups or Sunday teaching classes. All pastoral staff are *expected* to attend these same classes as examples to the flock, for personal benefit, and so they can turn everyday grace into the second nature of their home and work.

These are foundational studies that churches configured around small groups or Sunday Schools can greatly benefit from. What's more, these studies not only help parents grasp their role as gracious leaders of their families, but also help them develop a much more magnanimous view of their role in the greater work of the church. It's simple: grace-based people enjoy a deeper relationship with Christ and make a more profound contribution to what He's doing in their domestic church and local church. A gracious heart inclines people to participate more, serve more, and give more to God's work.

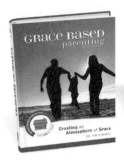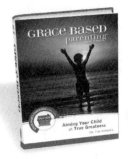

Resources: The *Grace Based Parenting* DVD series makes training in grace easy, fun, and transformational. For more information, visit *GraceBasedParenting.com*.

For training **grandparents** in the grace-based strategy you'll absolutely love the: *Extreme Grandparenting* DVD series. For more information, visit *Grandparents.FamilyMatters.net*.

3 **Baby Dedication.** Often baby dedication (for some churches: infant baptism) simply involves the parents coming a little early to a church service to find out where to stand. There's a better way to leverage this event. Because this event is so strategic and parents so desirous of it, it's a great time to require a single class that puts their role as spiritual mentors in a much bigger and biblical context. Our church already had this required class in place. It served as an excellent opportunity to explain the role of Jesus' truth and grace in their lives as well as give them an overview of the different ways the church was available to coach and encourage them as they raised their children (i.e., the different sign posts along the cobblestone path). Some churches use this class to assist the parents in creating the actual prayer or blessing that will be used in the dedication (or baptismal) ceremony.

4 **Give the Blessing to Your Child.** Dr. John Trent created a simple but powerful five-part blessing that can be taught to parents in a class setting. It becomes a great guide for them as they formally speak blessing into their child as well as informally bless them on an ongoing basis through their childhood. A good time to make sure parents begin this habit is in the 3-6 year old time frame. For more information on how to transfer the blessing to children go to *strongfamilies.com.*

5 **Love, Sex, & Honor.** Churches need to be encouraging and equipping parents to engage their kids in an early and ongoing discussion about love, sex, and honor. True, parents might be a bit nervous about the idea of beginning this discussion at the age of 5-6. Satan loves the fact that they are. He loves it even better if they assume that it's simply too early to introduce this subject. He's loves this for two reasons: He knows for a fact that it's not too early; and *he* wants to be the first one to introduce the subject to them—but he wants to tell them a bunch of lies. Satan knows that it is far more important to be first than it is to be correct. Being first gives him the high ground, and parents are stuck with trying to deprogram their kids through the remainder of their childhood.

A savvy grace-based family ministry takes leadership in teaching and equipping parents on how to introduce this subject to their children. It can be done in a one to two session class that puts the discussion in biblical context, deals with the standard "push back" issues, and gives parents ideas on how to initiate and frame this discussion. You'll notice the sign has an arrow facing into the future. This means that this is not a one-time conversation but one that starts around the time their children enter kindergarten and continues throughout the rest of their time under their parents' roof.

Some parents don't feel qualified because of their promiscuous past (one of the standard "push back" issues). Once again, Satan has to be chuckling. He loves using shame and embarrassment to silence Christian people/parents from doing what God expects them to do. But conscientious family ministries can give parents courage, clarity, and confidence to open up this discussion with their child in such a way the child feels safe to bring all of what they hear, think, and fear to their parents in order to find their way through it all. It's a spiritual crime how many children are brought up in Christian homes with little-to-no guidance on this critical dimension of their life. It's an added spiritual crime when churches do nothing to help them. As a seminary student, I remember my professor, Dr. Howard Hendricks of Dallas Theological Seminary, commenting on this issue of discussing sex with our children. He said, "We shouldn't be ashamed to discuss what God wasn't ashamed to create."

RESOURCES:

For the children *(available at Shop.FamilyMatters.net)*:

The Story of Me for ages 3 to 5. Stan and Brenna Jones. (Colorado Springs: NavPress, 2007)

Before I was Born, ages 5 to 8. Carolyn Nystrom. (Colorado Springs: NavPress, 2007).

What's the Big Deal? ages 8 to 11. Stan and Brenna Jones. (Colorado Springs: NavPress, 2007)

Facing the Facts, ages 11 to 14. Stan and Brenna Jones. (Colorado Springs: NavPress, 2007)

How and When to Talk About Sex. Stanford and Brenna Jones. (Colorado Springs: NavPress, 2007)

For parents who struggle with a disappointing sexual past:

The Sexually Confident Wife, **Shannon Ethridge (New York, NY: Random House, 2008),** *The Invisible Bond.* Barbara Wilson (Colorado Springs: Mulnomah Press, 2006). *Kiss Me Again,* Barbara Wilson (Colorado Springs: Mulnomah, 2009). Pure Hope at *purehope.net.*

6 Your Child's Uniqueness. Imagine sending your children out to play or to school every day dressed in fine clothes and sturdy shoes, but the clothes are two sizes too small and the shoes are always put on the wrong feet. Although they are well-clothed and have good protection for their feet, they're going to be very distracted as they go about their day.

This is exactly what happens in homes where parents fail to understand the God-made and unique design of their children. But how can they know? The bulk of tools for calibrating our unique personality bents are designed for adults. Fortunately, that's not the case any more! There is now a kit that plays a lot like a game that can be used with children as young as five years old. It's called *The Kid's Flag Page!* This kit gives the child (and their parents) a fabulous and clear picture of their unique design. This is a true game-changer when it comes to creating grace-based homes. This fun, interactive tool gives parents a wonderful look into the heart of their child as well as gives them clear understanding in how to parent them in a way that consistently brings out their best.

Resources: The Kid's Flag Page
KidsFlagPage.FamilyMatters.net

7 **Dollars & Sense for Kids.** It's never too early to teach the biblical non-negotiables about money. Money is going to make up a huge part of every child's future. It's best to introduce clear teaching on this as early as possible. With the right volunteer leadership and curriculum, this could be taught throughout their youth in several different ways. The key is getting their parents trained in the biblical laws of money and then showing them how to implement these principles with their children.

Resources: *Financial Peace Junior* by Dave Ramsey (Brentwood: Lampo Publishing, 2011). *Generation Change: Home Edition for Teens* (DVD) by Dave Ramsey (Brentwood: Lampo Group, 2010). This is a great parent-led DVD study (available at *DaveRamsey.com*).

8 **Rite of Passage.** Age 13 is a wonderful, mystifying, and often terrifying time in a child's youth. It's also a fabulous benchmark to touch their lives in such a way that you radically ramp up their ability to thrive through their teenage years. The Rite of Passage sign represents an *event*. It could be a trip to a place of the child's choosing or an activity of the child's choosing that is experienced with one of their parents (preferably mom with daughters, dad with sons). The key to this event is that you're drawing a line of demarcation in how you are going to view as well as treat your child on the other side of it. Going into it, you're viewing them as boys or girls. Coming out of it, you're going to view them as young men or young women. In preparation for this Rite of Passage event (or trip) you could have your child read a book on sexual purity. During the trip you'd want to set aside some pockets of time in the midst of your fun to discuss things like future dating, quality relationships, changes on the horizon, stepping up to greater responsibilities, etc. And then, when you come home, you let your teen know that you're going to treat him or her differently. You're going to give more freedoms and choices, but you're also going to give him or her more responsibilities when it comes to living mature and adult-like lives.

For kids who don't have both parents on board in their life or have parents who have yet to develop a relationship with Christ, the men's and women's ministry arms of your church could either come alongside the parents to help them fulfill this vital moment in their children's life, or, if the parents are simply uninterested, create a church-based event for them.

Resources: Robert Lewis has prepared excellent training in his book and DVD study *Becoming a Man: A Father and Son Adventure Together, Authentic Manhood, Raising a Modern Day Knight (rmdk. com)*, and *Men's Fraternity (mensfraternity.com)*. Another great resource is Dennis and Barbara Rainey's *Passport2Purity Retreat Kit* available at *Shop.FamilyMatters.net*. All of these resources give leadership in not only raising sons, but also how to mark their steps into manhood with strategic events like Rite of Passage. Women looking at this material could easily transfer the information into a female context.

9 **Your God-Given Gifts**. All kids have spiritual gifts. So do their parents. It's good to make sure that some time in their teenage years they get help in both identifying and developing skill in their spiritual gifts. Many churches have classes taught by a pastor or gifted layperson that can be attended by parents and teenagers together. Perhaps this is training that can come through the student pastor's department in your church. There are also some online inventories that parents and children can use that enable them to dial in on the unique spiritual gifts God has entrusted to them. Some of these online sites are better than others and all have their shortcomings. The best suggestion I have is to put "spiritiual gifts inventory" into your search engine and see which one comes closest to aligning with your church's and family's theological framework. The good news is that when parents and teenagers work through this exercise together, it gives both a better understanding as well as appreciation for how God is working in them and through them. This study of spiritual gifts, coupled with The Kids Flag Page, can give everyone in the family better tracks to run on when it comes to bringing the best out of each other.

10. **Lighting Up Your World.** If we are followers of Jesus, He expects us to be the light of the world. But the difference between wanting to be a light of redemption and hope and actually being that kind of light are often the difference between doing something accidently or deliberately. Your church's adult or student ministry may already provide training in evangelism. If not, there are many excellent books and tools available.

Resource: Because so many good people have created resources for training in evangelism, we're not going to create a long list of them. Most often, pastors or concerned parents already have a preference. If you're not sure where to start, one great suggestion would be Robert Lewis' DVD series called *Explore*. You can learn all about it at *LifeReady.com*.

11. **Ceremony of Manhood/Womanhood.** Age 16 is a standard line of delineation in our culture. Among other things, in most states 16 is the year a teenager can first legally drive. This is a great year to mark with a ceremony of manhood or womanhood. Notice that "Rite of Passage" is an event primarily involving one of the parents with the teenager. This particular occasion is more of a "ceremony" involving numerous adults who have played a key role in a son or daughter's life. It can be very elaborate, but it doesn't have to be. It might be as simple as inviting to your house (restaurant, et al) three or four godly adult friends and one or two church leaders who have played a key role in your son or daughter's life. You could ask these friends to share the one or two things they wished someone had shared with them when they were 16. Then have them isolate two or three extraordinary qualities they see in your son or daughter. Close it off by each one laying their hands on your son or daughter and praying a blessing over him or her and praying for their future.

Just like the Rite of Passage, some kids under the umbrellas of your church may not have parents who see or understand the importance of this kind of occasion. The men's, women's, or student ministry arms of your church could either come alongside the parents to help them fulfill this vital moment in their child's life, or, if the parents are simply uninterested, create a church-based ceremony for them.

Resources: Just like the Rite of Passage, you can glean a lot of great advice from Robert Lewis' excellent book and DVD resources, like: *Becoming a Man: A Father and Son Adventure Together, Authentic Manhood, Raising a Modern Day Knight,* and *Men's Fraternity.* All of these resources give leadership in not only raising sons, but also how to mark their steps into manhood with ceremony. The suggestions in these resources are easily adaptable to women.

(12) Preparing to Be Married. It's easy to think that the best thing we can do for teenagers when it comes to their relationship with the opposite sex is to give training in pure dating relationships. Unfortunately, this has proven to be a bit myopic priority. It makes more sense to put the discussion of their relationship with the opposite sex in a much bigger and lifelong context. Here's why. Many young people sabotage their future marriage simply by the selfish and foolish way they interact with the opposite sex during their dating years. Somewhere in the 14-18 year old corridor is an excellent time to do a marriage prep course geared to kids looking at marriage that may occur many years later.

This could be an elective offered to parents and their teenager on an annual basis by the marriage ministry department, youth or family ministry department, or by a gifted lay couple.

Resources: At this time, there are not many options for this type of training geared to teenagers. But the materials out there for adults could easily be used as an outline to create strong teaching. What's great is when this training can either come from or alongside the parents.

College Ready. It's no secret that the majority of kids brought up in Christian homes and who also attend church on a regular basis still have a difficult time maintaining a passionate commitment to Christ once they go to college. Many of them fall into deep moral holes or lifestyle traps. Too many of these young people come out the other side of their college experience with regrets and scars that often badger them all of their life. It doesn't need to be this way. What is vital is a parent/teenager study that can help the high school student see his or her college experience through clear and practical eyes. Fortunately, there is now an excellent curriculum to make this happen. This is a curriculum that can (should) be offered every spring semester of a high school student's senior year. All high school seniors (and perhaps juniors) should be encouraged to go through this study with their parents.

Resources: We highly recommend *College Ready* by John Bryson. Check it out at *CollegeReady.com*. Although College Ready can be put on by the church for just the high school students, many churches have found that one of the best ways to use it is to have both the soon-to-be-graduating high student along with his or her parent(s) listening to John teach the principles. Then, when they break into small groups to discuss it, have the students with one set of discussion facilitators and the parents with different ones. This helps both the student and parent to be more candid while still allowing them to work from the same set of biblical priorities as they head into the college years.

The Rest Stop Sign. You'll notice on the FamilyLand Map that there is a rest stop for single parents, foster/adoptive parents, special needs parents, and missionaries families on foreign soil. These are families that carry an extra amount of stress on them. A grace-based family ministry strategy can provide special teaching, help, and relief for these four categories of families. For the missionary families, it might be making all of the video tools and resources available to them free of charge and/or visiting them on the mission field with a team of people who are strictly there to encourage and build up their family's emotional and spiritual health.

In this same context, other ministries in the church can have a servant-oriented impact in these four families by bringing some of the man/woman power to bear on comforting, encouraging, mentoring, and helping these parents carry their heavier load.

Ongoing Training in Strong Marriages. Wise family ministry does more than just hope for strong marriages, it maintains consistent and looping training for marriages. LifeReady has *Marriage Oneness*, *LifeReady Woman*, and *LifeReady Man* (*available at LifeReady.com*). Two other great resources for strong marriages are Emerson Eggerich's *Love & Respect* (*LoveandRespect.com*) and Family Life's *Art of Marriage* DVD (*FamilyLife.com*).

A Volunteer-Led Ministry: None of the parts of this map require pastoral involvement other than he or she encouraging the lay people who step up to fill the gap. Because so much of the training is available through leading edge/cutting edge DVD curriculum taught by some of the finest family advocates and biblical teachers in the world, all that the full-time pastor really needs to do to have an effective family ministry is recruit and encourage the lay volunteers to cover these vital parts of this comprehensive grace-based strategy.

For excellent insight on how to unleash the power of your lay staff, watch the online video *The LifeReady Strategy* and *A Word to Pastors* at *lifeready.com/strategy.html*.

Two Final Thoughts Regarding the FamilyLand Map and the Grace-Based Strategy:

First: I want to give a huge thank you to the Family Ministry DNA Committee of Scottsdale Bible Church and Dr. John Trent for their contributions to the FamilyLand Map.

Second: If you want to gain a deeper and wider understanding of what God's grace looks like played out within the dynamic of families and churches, you might want to become a frequent visitor to the Family Matters website: *FamilyMatters.net*. Its blog articles and vast tools, including parents Q&A, are the "mother lode" for families and churches that want to not only partner wisely, but also do all they do within the context of God's amazing grace. My wife, Darcy, and I are regular contributors to the library of practical and biblical content. But there are also many other great thinkers and family voices weighing in from this valuable website. You can follow Family Matters through their blog, Facebook, and Twitter.

CHAPTER 10

PORCH LIGHTS

T hanks for investing your time in reading this book. We've been looking and learning together. Up to this point our discussion has been about how churches and parents can create a more deliberate dance with each other in order to be used by God to groom a new generation of passionate followers of Jesus.

Creating relationships within local and domestic churches that are guided by God's truth and tempered by His grace puts everyone involved in the best position to enjoy God's presence, appropriate His power, and realize His purposes. But there are some people who have been standing in the shadow of our discussion that I want to address before you close the back cover of this book. To do this, please join me on a road trip . . . .

The car had emptied out and finally, I was all by myself. About 180 miles up I-71 was home. It was a fairly new address for my parents as they had moved from Maryland to Ohio while I was in college. But even though the house wasn't the staging area of my youth, it still contained the people I most wanted to drive through the night to see.

Everyone would be in bed by now, deep into heavy R.E.M. sleep by the time I pulled in the driveway. Everyone, that is, but Mom. She said she'd leave on the front porch light. That also meant she'd be doing one of those things that only a mother can do. It's a combination of dozing, listening, and praying. The dozing part wasn't very effective but the intermittent rest it supplied would at least purchase her enough energy to make it through tomorrow. That's what you do when you have your college boy out on the highway on a bitter, winter night making his way home for Christmas.

I finished my last exam around 2:30 that afternoon. I'd packed the car that morning—a couple of pillowcases of dirty clothes and some snack food. Four other students had hitched a ride with me. By the time we were all ready to go, it was pushing five o'clock in the evening. I had been lightening the load along the way. One had been dropped off in northern Tennessee, two in Kentucky, and the last at a truck stop outside of Cincinnati.

That's where I had topped off my tanks and caught my breath. In my blue-collar mind, there are few things that compare to a crowded truck stop on a snowy night: clattering dishes, animation of short-order cooks, banter of long-haul truckers, biting cold that blows across your shoulders every time someone slips in or out, husky-voiced waitress with a pot of the finest coffee on the freeway.

It's on par with high tea at the Ritz to me. My last drop-off was a girl who sang off key to the radio. Her dad had treated me to a piece of apple pie, coffee, and some advice. The advice had something to do with staying the night at their place and finishing my trip in the morning with some rest and daylight on my side. Looking back, he was a voice of prudence. But it was Christmas. My family was on up the road, and there was a front porch light burning in the night just for me.

There aren't many things that can pull a soul through the night like Christmas. It draws folks through airports, train stations, and rest stops all over the world. It brings hurried hearts back to the hearth long enough to put some meaning back into their busy lives. I was no different. I needed to slip back into the context that had defined me from the beginning. I needed to be around the people who had given me life and given my life purpose—at least long enough to get my bearings and remind myself of who I was. Christmas can do that to you, even when you don't notice it happening.

Obviously, not everyone has Courier & Ives memories of their childhood Christmases. For some, holidays with their family is something they simply endure—along with the many regrettable memories. But for many, and for me, there was enough good about my youth that I felt I needed to finish the end of that year with my family.

That need for the touch of family drew me down the on-ramp and into the night.

It kept me awake when the inside of my car got too hot and all my fatigue rushed on me at once.

It kept me company when I couldn't find a decent station on my radio.

It kept me alert when the snow got heavy enough to accumulate on the road.

It kept me focused when I hit an occasional patch of ice.

My journey through the darkness was a small sacrifice for what I was getting in return. I had a family waiting for me who loved me and believed in the significance of my existence. We were all looking forward to collectively celebrating the birth of a Savior. The sheer power of an event so long ago helped me close the gap between my car and a front porch light. It slipped me past 18-wheelers, snowplows, and other nightriders. Many of them, like me, had a front porch light glowing for them too.

But, as I mentioned, for too many others, this night was a different metaphor. There were some who were just riding out the darkness. They were the ones who either hadn't heard or hadn't figured out what Christmas was all about. For them, Christmas was a department store Santa, too much eggnog, and a huge January Visa bill. All of this was unfortunate because the hope and the relationships waiting for me were waiting for them too. They just didn't know it.

They may have heard the story, but hadn't yet figured out the punch line. If Christmas is anything, it's summarized in lights. It's about a simple lamp in an austere stable lit by an anxious new husband so that he could assist his young bride as she gave birth to the incarnated God of Creation. It's about an overwhelming light that pierced the darkness surrounding some tired shepherds in bad need of good news. It's about foreign astronomers who followed a light across a continent to the threshold of hope so they could worship this divine child who had been born in Bethlehem.

Isaiah said it as well as it can be said:

> "The people walking in darkness have seen a great light; on those living in the land of deep darkness a light has dawned . . . . For to us a child is born, to us a son is given, and the government will be on his shoulders. And he will be called Wonderful Counselor, Mighty God, Everlasting Father, Prince of Peace. Of the greatness of his government and peace there will be no end" (Isaiah 9:2, 6-7).

The combination of a family that loved me and a God, who came to rescue me from my sin, was why a porch light was burning in the night in Ohio. It was burning because I wasn't yet home. The rule isn't etched in stone in all families, but for our family at least, the front porch light symbolized that someone, who lived inside that house, was still out in the night. As my siblings and I grew up, we knew that the last one in was supposed to shut off the light.

It was about 3:30 in the morning when I pulled off the freeway and covered the last few miles to that front porch light. Everything was just the way it was supposed to be when I slipped in from the darkness. I was safe because I was home. That's the power of Christmas. That's the power of family.

Several dozen Christmas' have come and gone since then. I've covered thousands of miles and passed a lot of folks along the way. Every chance I've gotten to chat with them on their journey, I've tried to tell them of the gift the Baby in the manger left for them. It took Him 33 years to wrap that gift and nail-scarred hands to deliver it. But it was worth the wait. He slipped through an empty tomb and went on ahead to prepare a place for us. We may have miles to go before we get home. We may have some lonely road and some nasty weather to endure, but for those willing to put their confidence in His work and His Word, there's a light burning on the front porch of heaven just for them.

LEAVE YOUR LIGHTS ON

As we've worked our way through the best practices for a healthy family ministry within our local and domestic churches, there have been some unspoken questions hovering in the back of our discussion:

- † What about those families that have the desire, but the setbacks of life (whether of their making or not), have made it extremely difficult to be able to embrace the opportunities a grace-based family ministry strategy has to offer?

- † What about those people who don't have a spiritual context to build from?

- † What about those families where only one of the parents has an inclination toward the spiritual pilgrimage?

† What about those kids out there who have parents that either don't have a clue or may even be hostile towards a spiritual heritage for their children?

One of the best ways for those, who stumble in the darkness, to ultimately find their way through heaven's front door is for grace-based homes and grace-based churches to keep their front porch lights burning on behalf of these people. It would be easy, because of the magnitude and urgency of these needs, to think our highest priority are these folks in the shadows and to configure our churches to primarily meet these huge demands. But that would be a mistake. It would put us back at a spiritual emergency room configuration. Although there's a place for an ER in the grander strategy, the best way to have a substantive option for the people who have little to nothing going for them spiritually is to have local and domestic churches that operate with a high degree of spiritual *health*.

That's why the best ministry we can have towards all of those people within our community, who are groping in the darkness, is to keep the porch lights of our local and domestic churches burning 24/7/365. The sheer example of God's amazing grace working through churches with emotionally and spiritually healthy families eclipses any emergency room programs put in place.

Kindness is attractive. Love is addictive. Grace is contagious. Hope is medicinal. When the spiritually wounded or lost people, who live among us, interact with grace-based families . . .

† By being our neighbors,

† Going to school with our kids,

† Competing in sports alongside us and our children,

† Working with us or for us in the marketplace,

† Enjoying camaraderie with us as friends over dinner or common interests . . .

It's like a porch light to cold and weary travelers.

When those same spiritually wounded or lost people follow the bread crumbs from these grace-based families to the grace-based churches they attend, they get to experience—perhaps for the first time—a religious context . . .

† Where the rank-and-file believers are actually doers of the Word and not just hearers.

† Where the spiritual air everyone breathes is set to a gracious temperature.

† Where the staff and volunteers not only work side-by-side for a divine cause, but also do so with kindness, respect, and honor for each other.

† Where the truth of God is graciously taught all the time.

† Where people's needs for a secure love, significant purpose, and strong hope are consistently met.

† Where the broken, battered, and bewildered are given the freedom to be different, vulnerable, candid, and to struggle.

† Where they observe professional leaders and lay volunteers operating from the strength of character defined by contagious faith, consistent integrity, practical poise, personal discipline, steadfast endurance, and inspirational courage.

† Where the rule, rather than the exception, are people who embody a humble heart, a grateful heart, a generous heart, and a servant's heart.

† Where they realize they've finally found a safe place to work through all of the dangerous junk within their lives.

The best advertisement for the gospel is a person who has been transformed by it. The way people know the gospel is what it says it is, is when they see its redemptive power bringing joy and purpose within the dynamics of otherwise knuckle-headed people living side-by-side with their knuckle-headed family members. When those same folks grow to understand the source of that joy and purpose within these families as well as connect the dots between what these parents are doing and what their local church is doing on their behalf, they are more inclined toward the greater reach of our churches than any evangelistic campaign or life-support program could provide.

This is why the antiquated models of the past must be replaced. We can't continue to accommodate church leadership that ignores the priority of family. We can't continue to offer programs that encourage parents to leave the spiritual heavy-lifting to professionals. We can't continue to prop up the notion that the most well-intended parent is simply no match for the carpet-bombing of our hostile culture. We need a philosophical starting point framed around the truth of God and saturated with the grace of God. We need churches that see their family pastor as an extension of the pastors God has placed over the domestic church, family pastors that are more than program directors. We need to employ family pastors with clear vision, encouraging hearts, and winsome ways who can coach their counterparts within these individual families.

More than anything else, the world needs to see the porch light of our grace-filled lives, our grace-based families, and our gracious-hearted churches. These lights, glowing in the darkness of a contrary culture, will draw the lost, lonely, confused, and disconnected people around us to the God who powers these lights. And that same power will be what fills our homes with transforming truth and irresistible grace.

The best thing churches can do for parents is to equip and encourage them to bring Jesus home. The best thing parents can do for churches is to bring a carload of family members filled with Jesus back to church each week. When God's truth, love, mercy, and grace are what is happening in church on Sunday and in our homes throughout the week, the world will take notice. Jesus said it would. He said, "Let your light shine before others, that they may see your good deeds, and glorify your Father in heaven (Matthew 5:16).

Grace-based churches and grace-based families are the porch lights along life's highways and back roads. They are those "Welcome Home" messages from our lives that we leave on for the hurting world surrounding us.

Once we finally figure out that God's grace doesn't need proof; it just needs practice, everything changes. Because as the great prophet Isaiah reminded us in 40:31, "Those who hope in the LORD will renew their strength. They will soar on wings like eagles; they will run and not grow weary, they will walk and not be faint."

Just think of all the incredible potential that will be unleashed for the kingdom of God when parents and churches work together to create a grace-based partnership.

FamilyLand.FamilyMatters.net

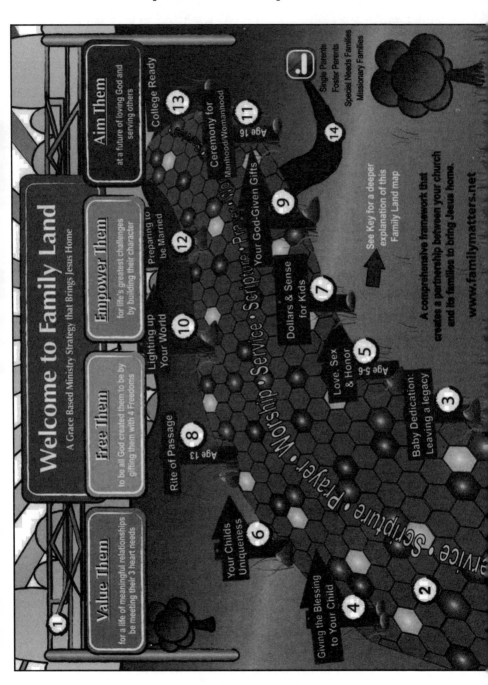

For a complete view and explanation, go to *FamilyLand.FamilyMatters.net*.

D6 Conference

a conversation. a platform. a gathering.

Bridging churches and homes
to the **heart of Deuteronomy 6.**

Connect with us online
D6conference.com

Family Ministry STARTS HERE

VISIONARY PARENTING

Readers of Visionary Parenting will capture a fresh, God-sized vision for their family. No matter where they are on the parenting journey, they will see God can transform their home. It begins with understanding God's purpose for the family and taking an honest look at the current state of the home. The author shares the foundational truth that God created the family to ensure that the next generation grows up to know, love, and serve Him. He reminds readers of the instructions from God given directly to parents in Deuteronomy 6:5-7 that will transform your home.

Visionary Parenting
by Rob Rienow
ISBN: 9780892655762
Price: $12.99

VISIONARY MARRIAGE

After years of counseling engaged and married couples, the Rienow's realized that most Christian couples did not have a biblical mission and purpose for their family. The couples had learned some things about communication, sexuality, and conflict resolution. But they didn't know WHY God had brought them together! Visionary Marriage will reveal that God does have a plan and a purpose for marriage and family in the Bible. The focus is on the big-picture purpose for marriage, and the goal of being successful once understanding the purpose.

Visionary Marriage
by Rob and Amy Rienow
ISBN: 9780892656042
Price: $12.99

Order today! D6family.com/visionary